Emotional
Well-Being

Praise for

Emotional Well-Being

"Dr. Neil Kobrin has taken a deep, piercing look at what it takes to dissolve our roadblocks to happiness. There is insight on every page."
—**Marianne Williamson**, bestselling author of *A Return to Love* and internationally acclaimed spirituality lecturer.

"In *Emotional Well-Being*, Dr. Neil Kobrin provides a very lucid and accessible integration of psychology and mindfulness for the general and professional reader. In his contribution to this conversation, the author includes personal anecdotes and illustrative case examples to show the relevance and intersection of these two perspectives. He makes clear the distinction between "our true nature" and the overlay of experience and culture which hides it and offers mindfulness as the process of recovery of our original condition. This book should get a wide reading from an interested audience."
—**Harville Hendrix, Ph. D.**, bestselling author of *Getting the Love You Want: A Guide for Couples*, and internationally acclaimed for his work with couples.

"Kobrin shows the positive and practical ways mindful psychology can benefit your life."
—Jack Kornfield, Ph.D., bestselling author of *A Path With Heart*, co-founder of Insight Meditation Society and Spirit Rock Meditation Center.

"In *Emotional Well-Being*, Dr. Neil Kobrin identifies the root causes of imbalance in our lives and presents a set of skills that can help restore balance. For psychological issues ranging from anxiety to emotional dependency, Kobrin offers practical advice for finding well-being which he brings to life through personal and archetypal stories. This is a book filled with beneficial insights."

—Phillip Moffitt, author of *Emotional Chaos to Clarity*
and *Dancing with Life*, founder of Life Balance Institute,
and Co-guiding Teacher Spirit Rock Meditation Center

Emotional Well-Being

Embracing the Gift of Life

DR. NEIL KOBRIN

NEW YORK

$\mathscr{E}_{motional}$ Well-Being
Embracing the Gift of Life

ISBN 978-1-61448-178-2 paperback
ISBN 978-1-61448-179-9 eBook
Library of Congress Control Number: 2011944159

Morgan James Publishing
The Entrepreneurial Publisher
5 Penn Plaza, 23rd Floor,
New York City, New York 10001
(212) 655-5470 office • (516) 908-4496 fax
www.MorganJamesPublishing.com

Art Direction and Logo Design
Jake Kobrin
jkobrinart@yahoo.com

Cover Design by:
Rachel Lopez
www.r2cdesign.com

Interior Design by:
Bonnie Bushman
bonnie@caboodlegraphics.com

In an effort to support local communities, raise awareness and funds, Morgan James Publishing donates a percentage of all book sales for the life of each book to Habitat for Humanity Peninsula and Greater Williamsburg.

Get involved today, visit
www.MorganJamesBuilds.com.

This book was written with love
and is dedicated to those who have helped
shape my life and influenced my journey.
Thank you.

Cover Story

Every spiritual tradition has stressed that this human life is unique and has potential that ordinarily we hardly even begin to imagine. If we miss the opportunity this life offers us for transforming ourselves, they say, it may well be an extremely long time before we have another.

Imagine a blind turtle, roaming the depths of an ocean the size of the universe. Up above floats a wooden ring, tossed to and fro on the waves. Every hundred years the turtle comes, once, to the surface. To be born a human being is said...to be more difficult than for the turtle to surface accidentally with its head poking through the wooden ring. And even among those who have a human birth, it is said, those who have the great fortune to make a connection with the teachings are rare; and those who really take them to heart and embody them in their actions even rarer, as rare, in fact, "as stars in broad daylight." [1]

Contents

Chapter One

The Gift of Life: Impermanence

Two waves in the ocean were having a conversation as they flowed toward shore. The larger wave was extremely depressed, and the small wave was peacefully flowing along. "If you could see what I see from up here," said the large wave to the small wave, "you would not be so happy."

"Well, what is it?" said the small wave.

"In not too long, we will crash into the shore, and that will be the end of us," said the large wave.

"Oh, that," said the small wave. "That's okay."

"What, are you crazy?"

"No. I know a little secret that tells me it's all okay," said the small wave. "Would you like me to share it with you?"

At this point the large wave is both curious and suspicious. "Will I have to pay a lot of money to learn the secret?"

"No, not at all," said the small wave.

"Will I have to meditate for thirty years?"

"No," said the small wave. "Really, the whole thing is only eight words."
"Eight words? Well, tell me, already."
"So," the small wave says, ever so gently. "You are not a wave. You are water."

Zen story[2]

Most of us agree that the gift of life is precious. We tend to love everything newborn: puppies, kittens, babies, etc. However, hidden in this lovely gift, the gift of life, is a tragic reality. You see, the gift comes with a *catch*, a catch so powerful that the fear of it influences our entire life experience. So, what's the catch? It's death! The large wave's worry exemplifies this fear.

Consider the biblical rendition of the creation of life in the book of Genesis: "Be fruitful and multiply, and fill the earth and subdue it; and have dominion over the fish of the sea and over the birds of the air and over every living thing that moves upon the earth" (Gen. 1.28). No mention of the catch. No acknowledgment that, at any given moment, without any forethought or warning, this gift can be taken away. This is what we all have to live with. This is the deal.

We may spend enormous amounts of energy trying to deny the deal, or forget the deal, or control the deal. We may develop a worldview, which may or may not include a religious orientation, designed to help us mitigate the effect of the deal. But in the end, the deal never changes. It is what it is, and ultimately we have to find a way to live with it. This is the challenge of life.

Social scientists have postulated that the very young don't seem to be consciously aware of this dilemma, and our awareness of it seems to emerge as we mature. Some debate whether animals have any awareness of impending death at all. But perhaps what we refer to as the "survival instinct," which exists in all species, indicates that this awareness does exist at least at a subconscious level. How else could we explain the purpose of an innate survival instinct, if it were not to preserve life? "Fight or flight" is a built-in mechanism designed for the preservation of the species. Even infants seem to possess this instinct, as demonstrated by their avoidance of crawling over dark shapes on the floor, which scientists interpret as a fear of falling through the darkness. If the deal didn't exist, there would be no need for a survival instinct.

So, what is the ultimate impact of this deal? On the bright side, we have life, a life that can be wondrous and glorious, even with all of its trials and tribulations. But the fact that this life can be taken away at any moment can cause us great fear, anxiety, and even hopelessness.

In fact, many psychological theories assert that the cornerstone of all anxiety and perhaps depression is imbedded in our fear of death, which generally resides in our unconscious mind. Anxiety creates an environment that supports pathology. In other words, the more anxious we are, the less emotionally healthy we are. This can lead to an array of negative behaviors.

One scene in the Woody Allen movie *Annie Hall* portrays a young version of Woody's character, Alvy. Alvy's mother has brought him to see a psychiatrist because Alvy is depressed. The psychiatrist asks, "So what seems to be the problem?"

"The universe is expanding," Alvy explains. "The universe is everything, and if it's expanding, someday it will break apart and that will be the end of everything."

"He's even stopped doing his homework," his mother says, with a look of total disgust.

"What's the point?" Alvy counters.

"What has the universe got to do with it?" his mother explodes. "You're here in Brooklyn. Brooklyn is not expanding!"

"What's the point?" This is the question that most of us ponder throughout our life. How do you live a life that has meaning, purpose, and perhaps even joy and revelry, knowing that at any given moment it can all end? What a terribly difficult challenge.

In his book *Man's Search for Meaning,* Viktor Frankl describes his experience during World War II while held captive at the Nazi concentration camp, Auschwitz. Frankl ponders the question of why certain inmates survived these horrific living conditions while others perished. He concludes that those who find meaning in life, despite the horrors of the camp, are better able to survive. He concludes that the meaning of life is found in every moment of living, and that, even in suffering and death, life never ceases to have meaning. Even in the face of death, the point is simply to live as fully as we can and experience the meaning of the moment.

Let's look at the deal from a different context. Imagine that your car broke down and you couldn't afford to replace it. Furthermore, imagine that you were desperately dependent on your car for your survival. You needed to drive long distances to find food to support your family. A friend, having become aware of your situation, decides to loan you a car. He says, "Use the car as long as you want; however, if I change my mind and want it back, I'm simply going to take it back. But don't worry about that. That won't happen for a long time."

The longer you use the car, the less likely it seems that your friend will ever take it back. You may even get lulled into a false sense of security that he will never take it back. Then one day, on a very stormy day, a day on which perhaps you should have never ventured out of the shelter of your home, off you go. In search of food, you travel further than you ever have before. You leave the car on the side of the road and begin your search for food. Several hours later, with the storm now raging, you return to the place where you left the car. But there is no car. It's gone and you're out there, all alone.

Most of us would never make that deal. We wouldn't want to live with the anxiety of knowing that we could drive off somewhere, only to get stuck because the car had vanished. We would try to negotiate better terms. We would likely be appreciative of our friend's gift; however, we would request that if our friend needed his car back, he would provide some advance warning, and we would make arrangements to facilitate the process. Seems reasonable, doesn't it?

Many years ago, I moved into an old Victorian two-bedroom house, which was occupied by a friend of mine who had been living there for several years. In essence, it was his place, which, despite the fact that I paid half the rent, relegated me to a "guest" status. One day he announced that he was offered a new job and would be moving from Northern California to Southern California. So the Victorian was all mine. I could either get a new roommate or not. I was happy for my friend. It was a good job and, although I would miss him, I was ready to occupy this house on my own. After all, we would still be friends, and given his connections in Northern California, we would see each other fairly regularly. Over several weeks, I helped him pack up his worldly possessions, and finally the day arrived when he climbed into his rented U-Haul and off he went.

As might be expected, I went through an adjustment period, but all in all, life was good. Indeed, my friend would come and visit on a regular basis. But after some time of this routine, I noticed that I started to feel apprehensive prior to his visits. I also became aware that I felt "funny" after he left. I didn't know what was going on.

One day, shortly after one of his visits, I decided to make myself some spaghetti. I boiled the water, poured the pasta into the pot, and waited the appropriate time for the pasta to cook. When my timer went off, signaling that the pasta was done, I grabbed the pot, went over to the cabinet where the pasta strainer lived, and, to my surprise, I couldn't find the strainer. I put the pot back on the stove and thoroughly went through the cabinet. No strainer. I felt an unusually strong emotional feeling that at first I didn't understand. Then I realized something. I realized that my friend, as had become his habit, took the strainer back to Southern California with him. I further realized that each time he visited, he left with various household items.

Technically, these household items were his, accumulated over many years of living in the house. However, they had also become part of the house, the environment, and I relied on some semblance of order or consistency in my household environment. If I needed a strainer,

I wanted the strainer to be where it always had been. I didn't like the surprise of not finding something I expected to be there. I didn't like the unpleasant feelings that I had developed toward my friend. The anxiety created in me by virtue of not knowing what would disappear next was more than I was willing to handle. I needed to find a solution, or I would wind up hating my friend and not being able to cook pasta. So I made a decision. I called my friend and said that the next time he visited, I would leave the house for two hours. During that time he could take anything he wanted. However, after that, he would never remove anything from my house again.

So, what does this story have to do with the "catch?" The issue I faced with my former roommate was not that I was losing my belongings; rather, it was that belongings would disappear without my knowing it, while I relied on them to be where I expected them to be. It was the "not knowing" that drove me crazy. Once I took control of the situation and declared that he had two hours to retrieve his belongings, I felt more in control of my environment. I could survey the house, make a list of items I needed, buy them, and live a more serene life.

In essence, this is what most of us continually do with life's challenges, particularly the challenge of death. We try to take control of the situation to ward off the anxiety that accompanies this challenge. We eat right, sleep right, poop right, exercise right, etc., etc. However, in the end, the result is always the same.

But wait—maybe we will live forever and this really *isn't* the deal. Just because no one has ever lived forever doesn't mean that it can't happen. We can hope, can't we? But this way of thinking can make matters worse. It denies the *impermanence* of life and the internal truth we all know— that it will end.

So if denial and taking control doesn't work, what is the answer? The answer seems to lie in accepting the impermanence of life and ultimately being all right with it. Only through accepting the impermanence of life can we ultimately lower anxiety and feel grounded in a way that allows us to live a quality life. It's good to eat right and exercise and bring a consciousness to your life that is helpful to your life's experience. But this cannot be in the service of immortality; rather, it is in the service of leading a quality life. Life is not about quantity. How long one lives is not nearly as relevant as how one lives. Everything is about the quality of the experience, the moment. *This moment is the only moment we have!*

This doesn't suggest that we lie down and die. This doesn't mean that we never again rail against the darkness of the night. What it does mean is that we recognize and accept the context of our life: the context of impermanence.

Every behavior must be viewed within the context in which it takes place.

Impermanence

The concept of impermanence is fundamental to many religious orientations, particularly Buddhism and Hinduism. The concept simply refers to the fact that nothing is fixed and permanent—hence the term "impermanence." This may seem rather obvious. But what may not be so obvious is the influence impermanence has on our experience of life. Buddhism asserts that there is nothing in the world that is fixed and permanent, and in fact everything is subject to decay. All things are therefore subject to change. The remedy to this reality lies in embracing impermanence. Hinduism maintains a similar view and basically suggests that the only way around this problem is to connect with the only thing that has permanence: our soul, which is eternal.

So how do we deal with impermanence? Often we simply deny impermanence and see things as concrete and permanent. And even when we accept impermanence, we believe that it is impermanence that makes us miserable and suffer. If only things were permanent and predictable, all would be well. Remember what the Woody Allen character said? "What's the point?"

But there is a different approach to how we can relate to impermanence. We can embrace the idea that we suffer because we believe things are permanent and *deny* impermanence. We can recognize that in an attempt to procure a sense of security, we "cling" and "attach" to things that we believe will make us happy. To provide us comfort, we hold on to these things tightly. It is this process itself that causes us to suffer because life is never fixed and everything is always changing. When we cling to things that provide us a sense of security, it is contrary to embracing impermanence.

The recognition that nothing is permanent can ultimately lead to a freeing experience, as opposed to our more common day-to-day experience of anxiety and fear. The Venerable Ajahn Chah, said, "If you let go a little, you'll have a little peace. If you let go a lot, you'll have a lot of peace. If you let go completely, you'll have complete peace."[3]

The process of letting go can be extremely difficult, but it can be done. The purpose of this book is to introduce concepts and methods to help us achieve a bit of emotional peace.

Letting Go

There is a story about how monkeys are captured in India. A hole is carved into a large coconut. At the top, the hole is just large enough for a monkey to place his hand into the coconut. The hunter places an attractive material, such as peanuts or banana, in the bottom of the coconut. The monkey approaches, places his hand into the coconut, and grabs a fistful of the material at the bottom. At that point, the hunter charges toward the monkey with a net. The monkey attempts to run away. However, his progress is slowed because he is dragging this coconut with him. If he would only open his fist and let go of the material to which he is attached, he could drop the coconut and run free.

Years ago, when I first started out as a psychologist, I had a client who was a 16-year-old boy. This boy was referred to me from a teen drug rehab center, after having been in the drug rehab program for twenty-eight days due to his drug-abusing ways. It should come as no surprise that he had a host of other problems as well, including a highly dysfunctional alcoholic family system, poor academic performance (he was on the verge of being expelled from school because of behavioral and academic problems), antisocial-type behaviors (swearing, fighting, cutting, smoking, stealing, etc.), and he looked like Satan himself (black leather with pentagrams everywhere). Clearly this was going to be a challenge.

My first order of business was to determine how I could best help this boy. In a situation like this, family therapy, or meeting with everyone who constitutes the family and working with all members of the family system, is often my preferred approach. I'm trained as a marriage, family and child therapist as well as a clinical psychologist, so the option of treating the family was viable. However, after my initial evaluation, which included meeting with the entire family, it became apparent to me that my best shot with this boy was to conduct individual psychotherapy. This approach has some inherent risks, which will be revealed by the end of the story.

One problem when treating an adolescent can be parental consent. Most often, the support of the parent is needed to begin the process. Another potential problem is the method of payment for services. Typically the parent pays the fee and not the adolescent. Traditionally, as I did in this case, I came to an agreement with the father regarding my fee and method of payment. Once a month I would bill the father and he would mail me a check. For several months, this method was successful. Then something began to happen. The boy actually started to improve. This was an arduous process of making strides followed by setbacks.

My approach was simple enough, which was to connect with this boy and simply allow him to have the experience of relating to someone who cared about his well-being and was not judgmental. Over time he began to embrace the concept that he alone wasn't the problem. He accepted and acknowledged that his "being" was okay and that his behavior was a reaction to many things that he had endured in his life. This way of thinking was not oriented towards absolving him from his negative behaviors; rather it was designed to separate his essential worth, his essence, from his conduct and the contributing factors that influenced his behaviors. As he started to emerge, there were fewer pentagrams, no more cutting, and generally he displayed a more positive attitude towards the world. Then something else began to happen. I stopped getting checks from the father.

At first, I approached this situation with kindness and understanding. I would simply resend the invoice, followed by understanding phone calls. The boy's father would assure me that he had simply overlooked the invoice or he was temporarily overdrawn, and I was not to worry, all would be resolved shortly.

After several months of this process, I realized that I had a problem. The father was not going to pay my fee. I started to become somewhat outraged. How could he not pay me for my services after the good work I had been doing with his son? His son was dramatically improving. Aha, *his son was dramatically improving.* How could I not see what was happening? I learned about this in my graduate program. Sometimes, when the "IP" (the identified patient, or the problem patient) starts to improve, it throws the whole family system into chaos. In essence, the family really doesn't want the problem child to improve. If the problem child improves, then the couple will have to look at their own dysfunctional relationship.

I was in a bind. Usually in this situation the only leverage a therapist has is to threaten to stop working with the client. This is supposed to motivate the family to re-engage. However, it was clear to me that this wasn't going to help the situation, and the thought of abandoning this boy, at this juncture, simply wasn't an option for me. Furthermore, I had only recently started my private practice and had only a few clients. I felt entitled to be paid for the work that I had done.

Every attempt I made to secure payment was unsuccessful. I even called a collection agency, which I had a legal right to do. However, my experience discussing this situation with the collection agency (of course without identifying the client) left me feeling like I needed to take a shower. It didn't sit well with me. The whole situation was troubling and upsetting and sat heavily with me. I felt ambivalent. I was very connected to my client and believed that he had great potential to turn his life around, and at the same time I was upset with how I was being treated by his father.

Then one day, on a magnificently beautiful afternoon, I took myself to the beach. The beaches in Northern California are a mix of rugged beauty and cold Pacific water. I walked for a while, looking for my spot—that is, the spot that called to me to sit a while and contemplate the world. And that is exactly what I did. Only this time I had a purpose. My purpose was to sit and meditate on the problem I was having with my client.

I spread my blanket out across the soft sand and sat cross-legged, staring at the ocean blue. I let the rhythm of the ocean waves lull me into a deep contemplative place and then began to concentrate on my breathing. I let whatever needed to come to mind come to mind, focusing my attention on the problem at hand.

At first, much of what I thought about was simply a rehashing of everything I had already thought about. But I refused to lose my concentration, and I continually refocused on my breath. Then something started to emerge, something that took me completely by surprise. I started to feel compassion for my client's father. Imagine that. This guy rips me off for a considerable amount of money and I feel compassion? That certainly wouldn't fly on the streets of New York City where I was raised. But, nonetheless, that's what I started to feel. I realized how unhappy and unfulfilled he was. I reflected on his life and how his behavior continued to cause him to suffer. And then I knew. I mean, I really knew, deep down in my gut, my soul, that I needed to let him go. He was not my focus; his son was. In that very moment

I let it go. I basically gave it all back to him. He would have to live with whatever decisions he made, and I really didn't have to be drawn into them. So, I got myself up, and walked back to my car with a new approach, a new plan.

During my next session with my adolescent client, I informed him that it was time for us to create a new arrangement. I told him that he had progressed well and that I believed that he was responsible enough to maintain his own therapy process. Now it was time for him to pay directly for his therapy and to leave his father out of the process. After a few moments of negotiation, we agreed on a fee of $5 per session, which he was required to pay to me each and every session. After our agreement, we continued to work together for quite a long time and he never missed a payment.

There is a footnote to this story. A few years ago, I was approached at the airport after returning from a business trip. A young man in his mid-thirties came up to me and said "Dr. Kobrin, it's [my client]." He went on to tell me that he was doing really well, that he was married, had a great position with a software company, and had two lovely Golden Retrievers. As for his dad, not much had changed.

What is important about this story is not how events turned out. What is important is the process I went through to let go of the situation to which I was so attached.

Let's quickly review what I did. I went to the beach, meditated, and voila, let go. Accurate, but not quite that simple. What I actually did was put myself in a nurturing environment. For me, that was the beach, with the warm sun drenching my body and the rhythm of the ocean calming me. I then concentrated on my breathing and the situation that had me so upset. Slowly, my whole body, my whole being, began to slow, as if I was entering another dimension of consciousness—and I was. I felt warm and secure and grounded. The anxiety of the situation began to abate. As it did, my perspective about this situation started to change. I felt compassion for this man, when only moments before I felt anger. I saw his life and his struggles and I began to understand that this was his journey, not mine. And even though I was impacted by his behavior, it paled in comparison to his life experience. As a result of changing my perspective regarding this situation, I was able to let go and find peace.

When you change your perspective, your attitude will often follow.

> *We who lived in concentration camps can remember the men who walked through the huts comforting others, giving away their last piece of bread. They may have been few in number, but they offer sufficient proof that everything can be taken from a man but one thing: the last of the human freedoms—to choose one's attitude in any given set of circumstances, to choose one's own way.*
>
> Viktor Frankl, *Man's Search for Meaning*[4]

Perspective

I recently had a powerful experience that will further illustrate this point. I was at a mindfulness workshop, and during a break I was seated at a table with one of my male friends from New York and two lovely Australian women: two different cultures and two different genders. The topic turned to crime and how it was different or similar in each country. My friend started talking about a negative experience that he recently had and how it affected him. He told the story of how someone recently broke into his car and stole his laptop. He went on to describe how violated he felt, and that if he had the opportunity to confront his violator, he'd love to do him bodily harm. Given the situation, this certainly appeared to be a natural reaction.

Then one of the Australian women began to tell her story. She told of an incident that occurred late one night in her driveway. Home alone, she heard a disturbance right outside her house. She went outside to investigate, and there she saw a young man, of Aboriginal decent, rummaging through her car. He had broken the passenger window to gain entry into the car and was searching for anything valuable he could take, or perhaps he was preparing to steal the car.

She approached the car armed only with a flashlight. The young man was so startled that he immediately exited through the broken window. However, in his haste, he sliced open a portion of his arm on the glass he had broken. Bleeding, he continued his ascent out of the car and was preparing to flee when she yelled, "Stop right there." Fear registered throughout his face and he was frozen, not sure what to do.

She continued approaching him, and then, in a rather calm, matter-of-fact voice, she said, "We can't have you running off with your arm like that. Let me get some bandages and tend to your arm, and then you can leave." She described his reaction as somewhat "unreal," not sure what he should do. But her voice and demeanor were reassuring, and he actually stayed put as she went back into the house and reemerged with bandages and medical cream. She tended to his wounds and said, "Off you go." No lecture, no harangue. He vanished into the night.

We were all listening to this story very intently. My friend, with his mouth open in astonishment, eyes dazed and confused, finally said, "How could you have done that?" This behavior seemed completely foreign to him and to the situation she encountered. Calmly, she explained. "This boy has probably been in and out of some form of jail for most of his life, and it clearly hasn't helped him. Maybe if, just once, someone showed him some compassion and kindness, it could have a greater impact on him and the rest of his life." By now all our mouths were open.

How could she have behaved so differently? How can it be that two individuals encountering a similar situation could react and feel so differently: one with rage (and warranted rage) and one with compassion? Perspective. His perspective was one of being "ripped off," taken from, and violated. And he was right. His reaction was consistent with the event. However, her perspective went beyond the event. She saw this boy and his life and his journey. Based on this perspective, her attitude towards him was very different. She was "mindful" of a larger issue, one that ignored her personal needs (protecting her possessions).

Mindfulness

What is mindfulness? "Mindfulness" is the English translation of the Pali word *sati,* which also has been translated as "constant presence of mind" or "awareness." (Buddhist texts were primarily written in Pali.)

Mindfulness has been described as a "calm awareness of one's body functions, feelings, content of consciousness, or consciousness itself."[5] It involves bringing one's awareness to the present moment, focusing on the experience of the mind and body. Through this process we can observe the aspects of our mind. We begin to notice a running dialogue in which our mind maintains a constant commentary about life filled with judgments and generalizations. We begin to notice how caught up we are with our thoughts and feelings, accepting them as a true representation of reality and believing that this is how things really are.

Mindfulness allows us to appropriately disengage from our thoughts and feelings by allowing us to recognize that 'thoughts are just thoughts" and "feelings are just feelings." They may or may not accurately depict reality. This helps us to relate to our thoughts and feelings differently and permits us to not be so heavily identified with either. Through this process, we don't have to be enslaved by our own thoughts and feelings. We can recognize that they simply exist in this moment, that they may not depict reality accurately, and that they will pass. This can be a very freeing experience.

Mindfulness has been characterized as "pure awareness," an awareness that precedes objectification, which is the naming of a thing or the identifying of a thing. Words are merely symbols that rest atop our awareness. Once our mind gets hold of something, it naturally tries to categorize it, placing it in a category that allows us to make sense of it. It would be wonderful to reside in pure awareness, or to live in what has been called the "empty mind." In time, with training, perhaps we can live in this state, or at least visit it at will. However, most of us have constructed lifestyles that make it very difficult to reach this state. Our cultural environment is not constructed to maximize this process. So what can we do to better understand mindfulness and incorporate it into our lives?

If we are to incorporate a new process into our lives, we need to understand what that process involves. Mindfulness can be understood and practiced on an ongoing basis. In his book *Full Catastrophe Living*, Jon Kabat-Zinn, a leader in the field of mindfulness, states, "Simply put, mindfulness is moment-to-moment awareness. It is cultivated by purposely paying attention to things we ordinarily never give a moment's thought to."[6] In a research paper written by Ruth Baer at the University of Kentucky, several authors are cited who collectively define mindfulness as "the awareness that emerges through paying attention on purpose, in the present moment, and nonjudgmentally to the unfolding of experience moment by moment."[7]

The basic tenet of mindfulness is "intentional" awareness of the present moment. We commit to paying attention to the present moment, to the "now." When we wander away from the present moment through distraction, or by thinking of the past or future, we gently return to the present moment. We train our mind to be focused on the moment and to be more of an observer than a reactor. When we are mindful, we are better able to observe and understand how our mind operates. When we are able to simply observe, and not judge or become overly attached to the moment, we are better able to quiet our reactive mind.

Mindfulness is actually like a dance between the observing mind and the reactive mind. In this dance, a "figure/ground" experience unfolds, where the observing mind is the "ground" and the event is the "figure" that takes place in relation to the ground. When the mind is calm, it is better able to be an observing mind, a mind that is nonjudgmental and unbiased. When the observing mind is truly focused on the moment and not influenced by past or future events, it has the power to regulate the reactive mind. The observing mind observes. It supports a present-centered awareness that is nonreactive and allows us to simply accept our thoughts and feelings without becoming reactive.

Reactivity is enhanced by stress and anxiety. The more stressed and anxious we are, the more likely we will become reactive. Show me a parent who has reacted to their child by striking them, and unless there is an unusual circumstance or the parent is antisocial by nature, I'll show you a parent who is stressed and filled with anxiety.

Mindfulness is not only being in the moment, but recognizing that the moment is all we really have. After years of doing psychotherapy with so many people, I know one thing for sure. The bottom line is that we feel how we feel in the moment. That's it.

Compassion

> *Within all beings there is a seed of perfection. However, compassion is required in order to activate that seed which is inherent in our hearts and minds.*
>
> The Dalai Lama[8]

The term "compassion" originates from the Latin word meaning "co-suffering." It is an emotional state in which we are able to access both empathy and sympathy for another's suffering. Our compassion allows us to be "openhearted." It allows us to feel deeply for another. Compassion brings us into our body and creates an emotional resonance that is felt deeply by us and often by others as well. It is a connecting experience. Not only does it connect us to our own feelings, it connects us to other living beings. Through the process of feeling compassion, we feel less isolated and more interconnected. Compassion is an emotional "attitude" that reflects a wish that another be free from suffering. Compassion is an expression of our love.

Compassion, along with loving-kindness, or the wish for the happiness and welfare of others, is the heart of Buddhism. The Buddha believed that the cultivation of both compassion and loving-kindness was the essential practice of Buddhism. When we are mindful, we are more able to cultivate compassion and loving-kindness, which in turn calms our mind and supports emotional well-being.

Self-compassion is no different. It simply means to be compassionate with ourselves. We tend to be so hard on ourselves, so judgmental. We are often filled with self-loathing and a critical voice constantly reminding us that we are not good enough or that we are not living up to our own expectations. This process undermines our ability to be emotionally healthy. If we can't support and love ourselves, how can we be emotionally healthy?

In the book *The Art of Happiness,* The Dalai Lama expresses dismay over the concept of self-loathing. He asserts that prior to traveling to the West; he had never encountered this idea. He believes that it is contrary to our true nature, which is a nature of "gentleness." He views all beings as being "precious" and affirms that we need to see ourselves and others this way.

Mindful Psychology

A new field of psychology seems to be emerging, one that I call Mindful Psychology. As I see it, Mindful Psychology integrates Western psychology with Eastern philosophy, Buddhist psychology, mindfulness, and neuroscience. This new approach can be very beneficial, because it can take the essential elements of all these disciplines and blend them into a theory that is very practical and much more kind and sympathetic to the human condition. We no longer have to be consumed by the notion that our unconscious or "true nature" is a dark, maniacal place, filled with aggressive and sexual drives that will lead us astray.

Mindful Psychology embraces the traditional psychological notion that emotional well-being is related to emotional stability and a balanced approach to life. It accepts that life is filled with moments of both joy and suffering and that how we react to either of these can influence our emotional well-being. It recognizes that we must maintain harmony between our rationality and our emotionality and use them in tandem to maximize our emotional functioning. It affirms that emotional regulation (our ability to manage our emotions) and emotional resiliency (our ability to "bounce back" emotionally after experiencing the travails of life), are essential elements that cultivate balance in our lives.

Mindful Psychology fully supports the Dalai Lama's view that our true nature is that of a gentle, compassionate, loving being. When we display unhealthy or, as Eastern philosophy would say, "unwholesome" behaviors, these behaviors are related to a reactive posture fueled by our fear or anxiety. Consider the potential emotional damage caused by a belief that we humans are hostile and aggressive at our core. These types of beliefs can significantly influence how we feel about ourselves and our worldview. Tell a child often enough that they are a loser, and often that is what they become.

Mindful Psychology supports the basic tenets of mindfulness: the intention to be fully present, and the recognition that this moment is the only moment we have. It supports being fully engaged in our life and embracing a compassionate, nonjudgmental view of ourselves. It supports the notion of the "Middle Way," a balance between self-indulgence and self-denial.

The intent of this book is to show how Mindful Psychology can positively impact our lives.

The Mindful Way

At the end of each chapter, there will be a section entitled "The Mindful Way." The intention of this section is to invite you to simply reflect on the material that has been presented or to participate in an exercise designed to heighten mindfulness.

A common acronym used at retreats and workshops oriented towards mindful transformation is RAIN, which stands for recognition, acceptance, investigation, and non-identification.

- *Recognition* is the willingness to see what really is occurring. It is the antithesis of denial.

- *Acceptance* is the willingness to accept the truth of how things are.
- *Investigation* is the willingness to look deeply into the experience.
- *Non-identification* is the willingness not to create an identity as a result of our experience, i.e., "I'm a loser," or "I'm a victim."

As you reflect on the material or participate in doing the exercises, I encourage you to keep in mind these principles for transformation: RAIN. I further invite you to be compassionate with yourself. Be mindful to hold yourself with loving-kindness.

The Mindful Way: Mindful Breathing

Breath awareness is essential to mindfulness. It brings us back into the body.

The breath is an indicator of our emotional state. It becomes agitated in anger, stopped in fear, gasping with amazement, choking with sadness, and sighing with relief.

The breath nourishes our body. Every time we take a breath, we fill our lungs and nourish our blood, which delivers sustenance to every cell of our body.

The breath can be a focal point and an anchor for our mindfulness practice. It brings us into the now and into our bodies.

- Find a quiet space where you are not likely to be distracted.
- Sit in a comfortable position, preferably upright with your back straight.
- Close your eyes.
- Take a few minutes to be still.
- With kindness, acknowledge yourself for being here.
- Bring your awareness to your breath.

- Bring your awareness to where you feel the breath most strongly in your body, maybe your nose, your chest, your belly, or somewhere else.
- Be aware of breathing in and breathing out—rest your awareness there.
- Feel the ebb and flow of the breath like waves in the sea.
- Notice the rise of the inhalation and fall of the exhalation. Just ride the waves of the breath, one inhalation and one exhalation at a time, moment by moment, breath by breath.
- Keep your awareness focused on your breath. Let any thoughts or feelings come and go. Notice them and simply let them go. When your mind wanders, gently bring it back to the breath.
- With kindness to yourself, give thanks for this time of coming back to the body, back to the now.
- When you are ready, gently open your eyes.

The practice of mindful breathing will help you heighten your overall awareness. You can do it anywhere, anytime. You just need your breath. In times of anxiety, remember to come back to focusing on the breath. Just tune into the breath or become mindful of the breath, breathing in and out. Don't analyze and don't judge. Just place your awareness on the breath: breathing in, breathing out.

A Solution Will Present Itself: Emotional Well-Being

In the Star Wars film *The Phantom Menace*, young Anakin Skywalker grows up enslaved on the planet Tatooine. A Jedi master, Qui-Gon Jinn, travels to the distant planet and, upon meeting Anakin, intends to rescue him. When his starship suffers an equipment failure, he becomes marooned on the planet. Qui-Gon Jinn decides to walk into town to find a salvage company in hopes of acquiring the engine part required to repair the starship and enable them to leave the planet.

Eventually, he locates a salvage company that has the needed engine part. However, the salvage owner, who is a very unsavory type, requires that he pay a rather exorbitant price for the part. Having no money, he leaves.

Discussing his situation with his home base, Qui-Gon Jinn is asked, "What are you going to do? You don't have that kind of money, and you may be stuck there for a very long time." The Jedi reflects upon his situation and says, "A solution will present itself." And it does. Qui-Gon

Jinn enters young Anakin in a podracer competition. He then places a large wager with the unsavory salvage owner, betting that Anakin will win the race—which he does. Qui-Gon Jinn collects the bet and pays him for the engine part. Together, Qui-Gon Jinn and Anakin leave Tatooine.

Emotional Well-Being

What does it actually mean to embody emotional well-being? Does it mean that we are always happy? Does it mean that we don't suffer the travails of life? There is a Buddhist principle that says each life is filled with "ten thousand joys and ten thousand sorrows." The meaning of this principle is that we all experience moments of joy and moments of sorrow. These feelings come and go, and we must remain open to the passing of each. Emotional well-being is reflected in our ability to embrace this principle, to know that life is filled with both happiness and pain. How we deal with these two ever-present experiences is a strong indicator of our emotional health.

When we maintain emotional well-being, we have the emotional resources to deal with both joy and suffering. They are aligned with our solid center, our emotional core, which allows us to go with the flow of life. Even when things are bad, we are able to withstand the painful aspects of our life. We tend to withstand the challenges of life without a complete deconstruction of our psyche. As Martin Luther King Jr. said in *Strength to Love*, "The ultimate measure of a man is not where he stands in moments of comfort and convenience, but where he stands at times of challenge and controversy."[9]

Generally, when we are talking about a person's emotional well-being, we are referring to their overall emotional functioning. The central qualities of emotional well-being are the ability to control our emotions and reactions (emotional regulation), the capacity to be in touch with our feelings (knowing what we feel in the moment), how easily we rebound after a difficult emotional experience (emotional resilience), our willingness to build strong and connected relationships, and our ability to lead a productive, fulfilling life.

In defining "well-adjusted" individuals, Drs. Ron Siegel and Paul Fulton in the book *Mindfulness and Psychotherapy* say, "They are resilient, richly filling the ups and downs of life while maintaining perspective. They are capable of close, loving relationships and are compassionate toward others. They are able to see things from multiple perspectives. They are productive at work able to identify goals and pursue them. They are aware of their strengths and weaknesses, and are not compelled to exaggerate the former or deny the latter."[10]

When we experience emotional well-being, we tend to feel good about ourselves and other people. We maintain a positive attitude about life, adapt to change, remain flexible rather than rigid, and create balance in our life. This is not to suggest that we don't experience the pain and challenges of life, but rather that we either "roll with the punches" or rebound more quickly when adversity hits. Mindfulness can help facilitate this process.

Emotional Resiliency

"A solution will present itself." These are the words of the Jedi master. This statement reflects a trust in the universe and a belief in oneself. Believe in yourself, be fully aligned with your intentionality, and the universe will often respond.

When we are emotionally resilient, we will weather the storms of life with greater dignity. When things go wrong, when life is challenging, we are better able to maintain our composure. This is not to suggest that our self-esteem, or our sense of worth and value, doesn't fluctuate at all. When life's traumas hit, we all tend to recoil. But when we are emotionally resilient, we bounce back. We tend to reestablish our self-esteem equilibrium more quickly, and we are not dependent on external factors to do so.

A few years ago, while preparing to go on a major trek through the Andes, I decided to have a complete physical, including a stress test to evaluate my heart. I had never had a stress test before. My doctor explained the procedure and then took me to a room that was equipped with a treadmill with an attached monitor.

After attaching several electrodes to my chest, I stepped onto the treadmill and the doctor started it. At first, it moved rather slowly, and it took very little effort for me to maintain my pace. But it kept increasing its speed and moved faster and faster. I could see my heart rate elevate and became concerned. For years I had used aerobic equipment and was aware that for maximum benefit you were supposed to bring your heart rate up to 80 percent of its maximum capacity and maintain it at that level for a period of time. As a result of my experience on these types of aerobic machines, I knew what my maximum heart rate was. As I watched my heart rate climb towards that maximum number, I couldn't help but think that this test was not going well. I simply assumed that the test was designed to see if you could keep your heart below its maximum level while engaged on the machine.

Eventually my heart rate climbed to its maximum level, and there it stayed as I continued to keep up with the machine. Minutes went by until, after what seemed to be an eternity (actually, more like five minutes), the doctor turned off the machine and pressed a button on the monitor where my electrodes were attached.

"Now, we wait," he said. We waited for several minutes as he occasionally listened to my heart and checked the readings printing out from the monitor. Finally, the doctor said, "Everything looks great." When I queried him about the results and about what exactly he was looking for, he told me that one of the key elements to this test is how quickly the heart rate returns to normal after having been operating at a maximum rate for a period of time. If I remember correctly, if the heart rate returns to normal (pre-test level) within three minutes of stopping the test, it indicates that the heart is functioning well.

If only we could create a test that measured our emotional resilience and our ability to repair our self-esteem in this way. The process of determining how quickly a heart rate returns to normal after enduring stress is analogous to the process in which we regain our self-esteem after enduring stressful situations. When we have high self-esteem, we bounce back, and we bounce back fairly quickly. When we have low self-esteem, we may never bounce back, and if we do, it takes a considerable period of time. We all face stress in our lives, and some of us experience real trauma. The more we accept and love ourselves, the higher our self-esteem, the more autonomous we are, and the more grounded we are, the better we are to handle life's challenges, regardless of how difficult they may be.

Emotional Regulation: The Vision Quest Story

In a Native American tribe, there lived a young man known as "Lone Wolf" who epitomized the warrior archetype. His tribe had a rich history and had been known to have the greatest warriors of all the tribes. Because of his great physical prowess, even as a boy, all were aware that one day he would become perhaps the greatest warrior the tribe had ever produced. Given his abilities and his precociousness, he received a considerable amount of attention and adoration, much of which went right to his head. He tended to be arrogant and egotistical.

As was the tribal custom, each young man during his thirteenth year was required to participate in a vision quest. Each vision was highly personal to the young man receiving it. Each vision carried a life lesson that would clarify what the young man would have to accomplish to reach his potential in this lifetime. Furthermore, this quest would determine whether the elders of the tribe would support the young man's elevation to manhood. No other event was as important to these young men as the vision quest. These quests would be discussed by the tribe for years to come.

The time came for Lone Wolf to engage in his vision quest. Tribal custom required that each young man journey to the sacred mountain and climb to the top to await their vision. They were permitted to take no food or water and could only enter the sacred sitting ground after they had removed all earthly possessions, such as clothing and adornments.

Although the climb to the top of the sacred mountain was arduous, Lone Wolf had an easy time making the ascent. He reached his destination by midday, disrobed, and entered the sacred sitting ground. As he had heard from stories told by the elders about their own personal quests, he emulated their behavior and sat cross-legged, closed his eyes, and went into a deep meditative place. Then he waited for his vision to appear.

Nightfall came, and he drifted into a deep sleep. Perhaps his vision would come in the form of a dream. But it did not. Early the next morning he arose, relieved himself, and resumed his sitting posture. The sun rose quickly, and soon the heat of the day was upon him. He waited and waited, but no vision appeared. By nightfall he was hungry and thirsty, and he could feel the strength of his body waning. Once again he drifted off to sleep. This sleep, however, was restless and fitful.

He awoke the next morning in a rather exhausted state. His resolve to continue his quest was weakening. His mind was playing tricks on him, trying to convince him that there was no shame in abandoning his quest. Now, fully immersed in his quest, he began to think that he was unworthy of a vision. It had been two days since he left the tribe. He was worried about how long he could physically survive without food and water.

By late afternoon of the third day, Lone Wolf had several hallucinations, thinking each was his vision and then concluding that none carried a vision's message. Finally, just prior to sunset, as Lone Wolf felt overwhelming despair, a vision appeared. The vision was of an old, wizened shaman. All knew of this vision, for it was held by the tribe as the most sacred vision of all visions. It came only to those who were the most worthy members of the tribe.

Lone Wolf had a surge of energy and couldn't believe his good fortune. All of his concerns and misery vanished in a flash. Dressed in a white flowing robe, adorned with a magnificent turquoise necklace, the shaman seemed to drift across the earth and approached the young man. "Rise, my son," said the shaman, as he extended his hand to help the young man to his feet. Tears of joy were now flowing from Lone Wolf's eyes. The shaman's face was aglow with love, staring deeply into the eyes and the soul of this young man.

Standing face to face, and without provocation or warning, the shaman struck the young man across his face as hard as he could. The blow sent Lone Wolf reeling to the ground. Enraged, he jumped to his feet and advanced towards the shaman. With fist clenched, he raised his arm to strike the old man. The shaman did not react, save to raise his palm to the face of the young man, and calmly said, "You may strike me if you wish, but know one thing if you do. It will be me who has control over your behavior, and you will not be the master of your own destiny." With these words, Lone Wolf paused to consider the wisdom of what he had heard from the shaman. He unclenched his fist, relaxed his tightened body, and smiled broadly at the shaman. As he did, his vision disappeared.

Years later, Lone Wolf became the greatest chief of his tribe. He had become famous, not for being a great warrior, but for being a great peacemaker. For it was Lone Wolf who united all of the tribes and brought peace and prosperity to the People.

Emotional Regulation

"You may strike me if you wish, but know one thing if you do. It will be me who has control over your behavior, and you will not be the master of your own destiny."

Emotional regulation is a primary aspect of emotional well-being. It means that an individual has the ability to regulate, to control, his or her emotions and the degree to which they are reactive. This implies that a person must maintain an appropriate amount of control over the impact that their thoughts and feelings have on their behavior and mood. They are able to regulate their emotional landscape and therefore are much better able to express a wide range of emotions and react in appropriate ways to emotional situations. They are attuned to their emotional life. They are able to recognize, analyze, and appraise what is happening for them emotionally and react appropriately.

When we lack the ability to regulate our emotions, much of our emotional life is out of balance. We may be highly reactive, reacting to situations in a more volatile manner than is appropriate to the situation. Or we may be "cut off" from our feelings and not aware of what is going on for us on an emotional level, and not react at all. This can lead to emotional restriction and can even contribute to emotional reactivity when we finally experience our emotions.

Practicing mindfulness is a significant support to emotional regulation. Through our ability to be aware of what we are experiencing, what we are feeling, and what we are thinking, we gain a perspective that allows us to assess and modify our behavior and our feelings.

Paradise or Hell: A Zen Story

Similarly, there is a Zen story in which a samurai warrior encounters a master and asks, "Is there really a paradise and a hell?"

"Who are you?" asks the master.

"A samurai," replies the warrior.

"You, a samurai? What ruler would have you guard his kingdom? You have a face of a beggar!" exclaims the master. The warrior becomes very upset at the master's insult and begins to draw his sword.

"So, you have a sword," the master continues. "It's probably too dull to cut off my head," he says. As the warrior draws his weapon, the master focuses on the sword and says, "Here opens the gates of hell." The warrior, taken by the master's words, sheaths his sword and bows. "Here opens the gates of paradise," says the master.[11]

When we are unable to regulate our emotions, and we react to our internal environment (our thoughts and feelings) or external environment with great negativity, we invite a "hellish" experience. Through the ability to monitor our emotional life, we reap the benefits of paradise on earth.

Emotionality versus Rationality

During many of the courses I have taught on the topic of psychopathology (the study of mental disorders), I have often presented a model that evaluates the degree to which an individual resides in their emotions or resides in their rationality. When we are emotionally healthy, we tend to have a balance between the two, even if we are more naturally oriented towards one rather than the other. When these are significantly out of balance—that is, when we are either much more emotionally dominant or much more rationally dominant—this can cause a problem.

More highly emotionally dominant people tend to have a lot of drama in their life. They tend to be very reactive and impulsive and often make decisions that are not in their own best interest. More rationally dominant people are said to be "in their head." They evaluate everything from a rational perspective and tend to be more emotionally restrictive, less "warm," more cautious, and generally less open.

When we are emotionally healthy, we maintain an appropriate balance between rationality and emotions. A major function of psychotherapy is to help create this balance: to help the emotionally dominant individual utilize their rational side, and to help the rationally dominant individual utilize their emotional side.

It is important to understand that either response, overly emotional or overly rational, is largely due to the level of anxiety housed within us. Both of these responses are defense mechanisms that are a response to internal anxiety. The overly emotional person doesn't have the wherewithal, or the conscious awareness, not to react. In fact, reacting is a relief, regardless of the consequences.

Consider the following. In 1989, the San Francisco Bay Area suffered a major earthquake. Despite the quake's magnitude and the devastation it wrought, there were very few fatalities. One fatality, however, seems specifically linked to an overwhelming experience of anxiety and the reactivity that followed.

A woman was driving her car on the upper deck of the Bay Bridge when, as a result of the quake, a span of the upper deck collapsed in front of her. The bridge is constructed of multiple sections (spans) that are interlocked to create a continuous roadway. As one would imagine, the woman sat panicked in her car, riddled with anxiety. This reaction was certainly appropriate to the event that occurred. However, what she did next cost her her life. She backed up her car, placed it in drive, and gunned the engine in an attempt to leap over the collapsed section, catapulting her to her death. Had she stayed put and tried to deal with her anxiety another way, she might be alive today. This may be an extreme example of reactivity due to anxiety, but it clearly demonstrates the relationship between the two.

What about the overly rational type? Have you ever known a person who lacks warmth and appears emotionally withdrawn or restricted? Or a person who lacks the ability to be flexible, must follow the original plan, and tries to control the environment?

There is a scene in the family movie *Beethoven* that exemplifies this type of behavior. The main character, the father, has a very important business meeting that could potentially change his life. He enters the dining room, dressed in a nice dark suit, and sits at the dining room table to eat his breakfast. After he is settled into his seat, Beethoven, his giant Saint Bernard dog, walks over to him and places his drooling head on his lap. Drool gets all over his suit. He reacts with disgust, pulls away from the breakfast table, and exclaims, "He slimed me." His wife calmly approaches him and says, "Don't worry about it". "I got dog drool on my pants. I can't meet with Vanguard Capital with dog drool on my pants", he bellows. "Honey, why don't you change your pants?" says his wife. Exasperated he says, "I'm gonna change my pants. You don't understand. I had a schedule, and now it's gone. I'll never have that schedule again".

What is important to this discussion is not whether we lean towards being emotional or rational. What's important is that we maintain balance in our life. For example, Buddhism encourages this balance through a principle called the Middle Path (or Middle Way), which describes a path of moderation between extremes. Essential to our emotional well-being is that we integrate emotionality with rationality to serve us through life's journey. Managing our anxiety, maintaining a calm mind, and developing "equanimity" (an even and balanced mind) are key elements that can lead to this integration.

Thoughts and Feelings

It is certainly true that our thoughts influence the feelings we are having in any given moment. If we are reflecting about something lovely that has happened in the past or are imagining that something positive will happen in the future, we are likely to feel good in the present moment. If we are fretting about something negative that has occurred, or are stressing about what will happen in the future, then we are likely to feel uncomfortable in the moment. There is a crude saying applicable to this process: "If you have one foot in the past and one foot in the future, you piss on the present."

Let's look a bit more closely at the relationship between thoughts and feelings. Imagine that you have a good friend, but lately you have been having trouble with this friend. In recent times, your friend has been less responsive to you and is always late when meeting you. As a result, you have built up a considerable amount of resentment. Each time your friend arrives late, you feel discounted and not important enough for your friend to arrive on time.

The two of you have made dinner plans. You are to meet at a certain agreed-upon restaurant at a predetermined time. Due to the recent problem you have been experiencing in the relationship, you are a bit apprehensive about this engagement. However, this has been a long-term friendship and you are somewhat ambivalent about your feelings. On the one hand, it bothers you that you have been treated in a manner that leaves you feeling less significant in this relationship. On the other hand, you feel somewhat petty about the way you feel, constantly trying to convince yourself that it's no big deal.

As is your pattern, you arrive at the restaurant fifteen minutes early and announce your arrival to the hostess. The hostess seats you at your table, and there you sit, awaiting the arrival of your friend. The minutes tick by, and at the prearranged time your friend once again does not arrive. You take a breath and decide to give your friend a reasonable leeway of twenty minutes. Twenty minutes comes and goes. You get up from the table and decide to leave. However, the thought crosses your mind that if you don't wait for your friend and confront this situation, you never will. You sit yourself down, fuming, and wait. Thirty minutes goes by, then forty, then fifty, and finally one hour after the prearranged time, your friend walks in. You are furious and prepared to share your fury.

Your friend arrives at the table and says,

"Please, before you say anything, let me explain. I know that I have been less of a friend to you than I should be, or than I have been in the past. I know that I have been late to everything we have done together, and I could sense that this has been bothering you. And frankly, it has been bothering me as well. So much so, I have been working on this very issue with my therapist, trying to understand what's going on with me.

"This night was to be different. I left my house an hour and a half early, not only to get here on time, but to get here early enough to buy you flowers from the vendor next door and apologize for my behavior. As I was driving here, there was a horrible accident on the freeway, right in front of me. A young lady was killed in a head-on collision with a drunk driver. It's all over the news. Right in front of me! I got out of my car and I saw her there, just lying lifeless in this totally smashed-up car. It was horrific. The cops came and closed down the freeway while the ambulance took her away, as well as the other guy who apparently suffered only minor injuries. I'm so sorry, and I will make every effort to treat you better in the future."

How do you think your earlier feelings of rage and fury may have changed as a result of what was said? I would imagine that your emotions would have changed considerably: from rage to compassion, from fury to appreciation. But what actually occurred to change your emotions? You simply received new information. This information influenced your thoughts and changed the context in which you experienced your friend's behavior, which then guided you to feel another way.

This process works in reverse too. That is to say, how you feel in any given moment can skew your thoughts considerably. People who are depressed have far more negative thoughts than people who are not, regardless of the information they receive from the world.

Here is a little trick that can help distinguish feelings from thoughts. If we can replace the word "feel' in a sentence with the word "think," and the sentence is grammatically correct, then we are most likely having a thought, not a feeling. For example, consider the following sentence. "I feel that you don't love me." If we replace the word "feel" with the word "think," the sentence will read as follows: "I think that you don't love me." As you can see, this sentence is grammatically correct. Therefore, we have had a thought, not a feeling. Let's try it in reverse. Consider the following sentence: "I feel sad." Replace the word "feel" with the word "think," and it is not a grammatically correct sentence: "I think sad." People often confuse their thoughts with their feelings and their feelings with their thoughts. This trick is a simple way to keep them straight.

Feeling Context

Emotions have a contextual base. Emotions spring forth from a feeling context that is either anxious or non-anxious, and this context can vary by degrees of intensity. An anxious feeling context will elicit certain emotions that will be different than a non-anxious feeling context. The intensity of these feelings will depend on the level of anxiousness. In other words, emotions stem from a feeling context that is either anxious or non-anxious, and this context exists on a continuum from mild to intense. Below is a sample list of emotions that can be elicited based on the feeling context:

Anxious Feeling Context	Non-anxious Feeling Context
Anger	Joy
Aversion	Love
Hate	Compassion
Insecurity	Calm
Fear	Happiness
Paranoia	Security

Essentially our feeling context sets the stage for the type of emotional experience we will have. If we are in a non-anxious, calm place, we are much more open to experiences of joy, happiness, love, compassion, serenity, and security. If we are in an anxious place, we are much more prone to emotions such as anger, fear, hatred, paranoia, aversion, and insecurity.

As adults we can influence this process. For example, our environment may impact us negatively and move us into an anxious place. However, we have the capacity to alter our environment in such a way to move us into a non-anxious place. By environment I do not only mean our external environment, but our internal environment as well, our thoughts and feelings. We may begin in an anxious place, but because of certain actions we take, such as calming the body through breathing, or becoming aware of our thought patterns and simply observing them rather than engaging them (being mindful), or exercising, or communing with nature, or connecting deeply with someone, we can move into a space of non-anxiousness.

The difference between us as adults and us as infants is that we have the capacity to move ourselves into a different emotional space. Infants are dependent on their external environment to make the shift from an anxious place to a non-anxious place, while we, as adults, are not. We can learn methods that can help us shift from an anxious place to a non-anxious place. We can change the way we feel by virtue of what we do to move us to a place of equanimity, an evenness of mind that is balanced and centered.

Eastern philosophy takes a similar view of this process and talks about primary feelings and secondary feelings. Primary feelings are feeling tones that are either pleasant (non-anxious), painful (anxious), or neutral. Secondary feelings arise out of these feeling tones and create the emotional fabric of our life. Through practicing mindfulness, we can work with these feelings to modify the power they hold over our life experience.

When our emotions result from a non-anxious feeling context, we are expansive. We expand into experiences such as happiness, calm, and love. When our emotions result from an anxious feeling context, we contract, which leads to experiences based in fear and anxiety.

The Mindful Way: Emotional Regulation

- Close your eyes.
- Bring your awareness to your breath.
- Bring your awareness to where you feel the breath most strongly in your body—maybe your nose, your chest, your belly, or somewhere else.
- Just be aware of breathing in and breathing out—rest your awareness there.
- Now bring your awareness to an experience in which you were emotionally reactive. Allow yourself to experience this event in the present moment. Let yourself simply feel the experience.
- *Recognize* the emotion that you are feeling, i.e., anger, fear, etc.
- *Accept* this emotion. Do not judge it or censor it.
- *Investigate* this emotion. Explore the emotion. What indication tells you are experiencing this emotion? Where do you feel it in your body? What does it feel like?

- *Non-identify* with this emotion. Say to yourself, "This is not who I am. This is simply something I am feeling."
- Now imagine yourself dealing with this situation differently. Imagine that you are simply an observer of these events. What do you see? How does this view change your perspective? How does it feel? Let yourself simply feel the experience.
- When you are ready, simply open your eyes.

The next time you find yourself reacting to a situation, recall this experience. Change your view of the situation from a participant to an observer. Let yourself center in your body. Take a breath, and let a cooler mind prevail.

Chapter Three

The Maybe Story: Nonattachment

Once there was a farmer who had worked very hard for many years. Although not wealthy, he had a son and a horse. One day his horse ran away. News traveled quickly to the farmer's neighbors, who chose to pay him a visit and console him about his horse. "Such bad luck," they said with warmth and sympathy.

"Maybe," responded the farmer.

Soon afterwards the farmer's horse returned, along with three wild horses, increasing the farmer's herd considerably. The neighbors paid the farmer another visit, and this time with joy in their hearts, said, "How wonderful that your horse has returned and you now have such a large herd."

"Maybe," responded the farmer.

The next day the farmer's son decided to ride one of the wild horses. He was quickly thrown from the horse and broke his leg. The

neighbors came again and offered their condolences to the farmer.
"Such a terrible misfortune," they said.

"Maybe," responded the farmer.

Soon the government went to war and sent military officials
to all of the farms to enlist all of the young men into the army.
Discovering that the farmer's son was injured, they let him be.

The neighbors were elated by the news that the young man was
spared from going to war, and once again they visited the farmer
and congratulated him on how well everything worked out.

To which the farmer replied, "Maybe."

Taoist story[12]

In the story above, the farmer exemplifies embracing impermanence and not becoming attached to his current set of circumstances. He knew that life was continuously changing, and we can't put too much credence in either positive or negative events. As hard as we try, we simply cannot predict the future. Our challenge is to stay present in the moment. The moment is all we really have. Mindfulness can help us achieve this.

Nonattachment versus Attachment

Imagine that the concept of mindfulness is similar to the experience of viewing a movie. What actually occurs when we view a film? Images are projected onto a screen, and, without us being aware of it, our observing mind identifies and categorizes these images to make sense of them. The result of this process is an experience. That is to say, based on the observing mind's interpretation of these images, we have an emotional experience. If it is a good movie, we are more likely to be fully engrossed in the film. We are in the state of "being in the moment." We are likely to experience strong emotions. Whether these emotions are joy or sadness or simply "fun," we have an emotional response. If we experience the movie as a "bad" film, we are more likely to be less present in the moment, our mind wandering away from the film and our emotional response lessened.

However, a movie is not real. It is simply images made up of several film frames projected onto a screen. It's one dimensional; it's flat. If you throw a rock at it, you tear the screen and nothing more. However, when we experience these multiple film images, we have an emotional response just like we do when we experience anything in our actual world. So, wherein lies the difference between the experience we have while viewing a film and the experience we have participating in "real life?" The answer lies in the context in which we have the experience.

The context in which we experience a motion-picture film is one of nonattachment. The mind knows that, regardless of the power of the experience, it's just a film; it's not real. This creates a nonattached experience, an experience I like to call "nonattached engagement." I would argue that by virtue of the nature of the context (one of nonattachment), our mind permits us to be more fully engaged, hence, "nonattached engagement." Many of us have more powerful emotional experiences viewing a film than we do in real life. Why? Because the process of nonattachment allows us to be more fully engaged with the motion-picture experience. Our mind doesn't create a barrier of protection because we are afraid to be hurt or wounded by the film. In fact, we know that if we don't like the film, we can simply walk out. This leaves us free and open to experience the film more fully.

When our world is shaped by how others feel about us, or by the number of toys we possess, or by how much fame or fortune we have, we are shackled to them. We hold tight to them, and the more we have, the tighter we hold. These things provide external validation, and we often create a dependence on them to allow us to feel good about ourselves. However, when we release the things to which we are most attached, such as others liking us or seeing us in a particular way, or possessing things that make us feel good about ourselves, or even our own accomplishments, then we are truly free to connect.

External Validation

To understand the power of external validation, consider the following research.

Some years ago, a study was conducted with children to measure the effects of external validation versus internal validation on their behavior. External validation is relying on someone else to make you feel validated, or feel good about yourself. Internal validation is feeling good about yourself without the need for social cues to reinforce that feeling. A group of volunteer parents were asked to assemble a few of their child's favorite toys and take them to a children's center. The toys were displayed in a large playroom that was equipped with a viewing window.

For several days, the parents brought their child to the playroom, and the children were left on their own to play with their toys. Outside the viewing window, researchers recorded the amount of time that each child played with each of their favorite toys. After a baseline was established (the average amount of time spent by each child with each toy), the researchers intervened by validating each child when the child played with the toy. They did this by administering both praise and candy each time the child played with the toy. They then established a new baseline and, as expected, the amount of time spent by each child playing with each toy increased some.

Then the intended intervention took place. The researchers stopped validating the children for playing with their toys. And what do you think happened? The children stopped playing with their favorite toys. Once the shift was made from an internally focused process ("I love my toy because I enjoy playing with it") to an externally focused process ("I love my toy because I get praise and candy every time I play with it"), the children lost interest. This wasn't a conscious process. The toys simply lost their appeal. The power of external validation was too great, and the children felt the loss when it was removed—just as you and I do when our system of external validation is removed.

Look at our education system. What is it based on? In a desire to motivate our children to learn, we have constructed a system that is based on external validation in the form of grades. As a result, we tend to emphasis grades rather than the cultivation of an engaged, stimulating, learning environment. This is why there are certain private schools that take a whole different approach to education, ones that are much more focused on creating a learning environment based on internal validation. The act of learning appears to be inherently joyous. Watch an infant learn something new, or master something they have been working on for a while. They experience pure delight. But often when we "attach" something to this process (such as grades), we seem to contaminate it.

I would like to tell you a story about Leo Buscaglia, widely known as Dr. Love. Leo was an author, a motivational speaker, and a professor, and he taught a course at the University of Southern California called Love 1A. He deeply believed that love and connectedness were the keys to leading a fulfilling life and talked about the barriers we create that prevent them from occurring. He believed in the power of touch, and often long lines would form after his lectures just to get a hug from Leo. Years ago, I saw Leo speak. He was talking about the value of love and what can interrupt the flow of love between people.

In this lecture he concentrated on stress, and how the more stressed a person is, the less available they are to love. He talked about his own journey to success and the impact that it had on his life. He described a time in his professional life when he had very little. He had little money, rented an apartment, and drove an old beat-up car. What money he had, he used to travel. He loved to travel because it allowed him to connect to the people of the world. Then something happened. Thanks to a TV series produced by the Public Broadcasting System, Leo became famous.

Fame and fortune started to build. Leo junked his car and bought a new one, moved out of his apartment and bought a beautiful house with a big lawn, and filled his house with all the things he could never afford to buy in the past. Every weekend he proudly mowed his lawn along with his fellow neighbors, who also participated in this ritual. However, Leo began to realize something. He had become more concerned about his material things than about his freedom to explore the world. Leo was traveling less. Furthermore, it had become more complicated to simply pack up and go. Who would watch the house? Who would water the lawn and cut the grass? Who would feed the cats? Who would look after his worldly possessions? Leo's stress was mounting. His things were becoming more important than his life experience. Leo became "attached."

The good news about this story is that Leo came to realize the error of his ways. He eventually had the awareness to understand what he was doing and the trap he had built for himself. He had become tied to his things. So one day, Leo set it all ablaze.

Not really, but it sure sounds good for the story. However, Leo did do something dramatic. Leo became aware of his attachment and, through this awareness, decided to change his perspective. He put his things, metaphorically speaking, in their proper place. They were things. Yes, perhaps they made life a bit more comfortable or even more enjoyable, but compared to having the freedom to go and be in the world, to be available to connect to people and to life, they had become his chains. He would not allow them to dictate his life any longer. If he lost them, he lost them. Leo Buscaglia became nonattached.

Nonattachment

Nonattachment, viewed within a context of awareness and mindfulness, reflects an emotional state in which an individual is not attached to the concepts of the world (or a worldview) or to life's possessions, accomplishments, or relationships as a *means of fulfillment*. It is a mindful state, a state in which one is more an observer than a reactor. It is a state in which one can attain a heightened perspective about life and the events that unfold on a daily basis. Mindfulness can be seen as embracing the observing mind and quieting the reactive mind. Nonattachment supports the separation of one's thoughts from the reactivity these thoughts generate. Our inability to monitor and observe our thoughts, and maintain a figure-ground relationship between our thoughts and our feelings, is what causes disharmony and stress.

Think back to chapter 1 and the different ways our two victims of car break-ins reacted. One was furious, angry, and vengeful. The other felt compassion and concern. How can two similar events cause two completely different responses? The answer perhaps lies in the context, or the actual state of mind, in which each person experienced these events.

It is said that "beauty is in eye of the beholder." In fact, everything we witness, all perceptions, are in the mind of the beholder. A nonattached, non-reactive mind will see things and experience things differently. This mind will experience the event from a heightened perspective. Somebody breaking into your car and stealing from you may indeed deserve a reaction of anger and fury. However, how does this response help you? Your heart rate goes up, your stress is increased, your fear and anxiety is heightened, and your mind is anything but quieted. But if you can take a step back, take a breath, and perhaps see the larger picture, your response can change. If you see what may have led up to the action that affected you, without being attached to your reaction, you may be able to garner some compassion and completely change your whole experience.

From the perspective of nonattachment, it is attachment that causes us pain. The gurus and sages tell us that the true form of nonattachment begins with "empty mind" (Samadhi)—the no-mind, the no-thoughts. This is simply a state of "being," a state without categorization. Perhaps this state, through much practice and meditation, can be realized. However, I believe that there can be a middle ground, a mindful realm, in which we are aware of our attachments and consciously detach from them on an ongoing basis.

This can seem to be a confusing message. We are attached to our possessions. We are attached to our relationships. We are attached to our constructs. We are simply attached. Most of us crave engagement and yearn for a connection with other living things. This is certainly not the "empty mind" that the sages and gurus talk about. However, perhaps there are different forms of attachment. Feeling connected to or engaged with another human being is a wonderful experience and doesn't necessarily constitute the type of attachment that has to cause suffering. However, if your self-worth, or your happiness or fulfillment, is dependent on these connections, then you are vulnerable to the pain and suffering that attachment brings. The less you need external validation, or the more nonattached you are from needing these connections to validate you, the freer you are to fully embrace these connections.

An extreme example of the true meaning of nonattachment can be seen in the rather bizarre movie entitled *El Topo*. This movie centers on one man's journey to reach his full potential, to become the "best." Of course, reaching your full potential as a human being and becoming the best at something are two very different processes. The need to become the best exemplifies attachment, because it suggests that one can feel fulfilled only if one achieves the status of "the best." In any case, this man sets out on a rather bizarre journey in which he would have to defeat four masters to reach his goal. Because our hero is, in fact, a gunslinger, and his journey is to become the best, one might conclude that the film could be called a Western. But this film is far from the genre of cowboys and Indians.

After overcoming all of the challenges our hero had to confront, he arrives at his final challenge. Standing in the arid, dry desert, he is faced by a small, partially naked, skinny, disheveled old man, armed with a butterfly net. The hero's task is to defeat the old man in a gun duel. But the old man has no gun, so he tells the gunslinger that he will have to fight him in hand-to-hand combat. Our hero strikes, but the old man is too quick and agile. Strike after strike finds nothing but air. Finally, in complete frustration, our hero draws his gun and fires upon the old man. The old man reacts with lightning speed and uses his butterfly net to deflect the bullet so it causes him no harm. He then says, "You see my net is mightier than your bullets. If you shoot again, it will go back into your heart."

Distraught, the gunslinger falls to his knees. "How could you win?" asks the old man. He then says, "Even though you cheated, you couldn't have taken anything." The gunslinger responds and says, "Yes, I could have taken your life." The old man, with a smile on his face, says, "Life, I don't care about that. I'll show you." He takes the gunslinger's gun and shoots himself. As he is dying, he says, "You lost."

The old man in this story represents the archetypical sage, aligned fully with spirit, and not even attached to life itself.

But how does this help the average person? How does this help us to feel better about ourselves, to become less reactive, and to move to a more compassionate, loving place in the world? Do we truly have to reach Nirvana? Do we have to give up all of our worldly possessions and walk the earth on a spiritual journey, as did Siddhartha (the Buddha)? I'm sure that this would be a most glorious space in which to reside: pure spirit, pure energy. But there must be a middle ground, an emotional space that is healthy and leads us more towards contentment and less towards anguish. I believe that by reducing our anxiety, becoming less attached, and coming to grips with the "deal" by embracing impermanence, this place can become more accessible to us.

The less attached we are to our possessions, accomplishments, relationships, etc., the more open we become to fully experience them. But what about the fact that, unlike viewing a film, real life experience can hurt us? Of course real life can hurt us. However, much of the hurt and suffering we experience is a result of our attachments. We often want or need something from our attachments, such as validation or stimulation. When what we desire or anticipate receiving is withheld or not forthcoming, we suffer.

Suffering: A Buddhist Perspective

I teach about suffering and the way to end it.

The Buddha

Since mindfulness is based on Buddhist philosophy, it may be helpful to have some understanding of the history of Buddhism and its relation to emotional well-being.

Buddha, known originally as Siddhartha Gautama, was born into a wealthy noble family. Some say his father was a king and he a prince. Upon his birth, it was prophesized that he would either become a king or a great holy man. His father, in an attempt to ensure that he would be a king, sheltered Siddhartha and provided him with all the comforts and safety wealth could provide. As a result, Siddhartha spent a life of luxury within his father's vast palace compound. He married and had a child.

However, Siddhartha grew restless and discontent. One day, at age twenty-nine, accompanied by his servant, he left the palace to see how the surrounding villagers lived. During his sojourn, he encountered what has been referred to as the "Three Divine Messengers": someone ill, someone old, and a dead body. (Some texts add a fourth messenger, a monk who lives as a renunciate.) Upon his return to the palace, he told his father that he intended to leave to seek out an understanding of the suffering of life. His father said he would do anything to make him stay. So Siddhartha said, "If you can promise me three things, then I will stay. Promise me that I will not become ill, age, or die." Of course, the king could not promise any one of these, so Siddhartha left the palace.

Believing it to be the best way to understand the issues of the human condition, he became an ascetic, or "a person who dedicates his or her life to a pursuit of contemplative ideals and practices extreme self-denial or self-mortification for religious reasons." After six years of this practice and nearly dying from starvation, Siddhartha abandoned this way of life. Instead he decided to meditate beneath what became known as the

"Bodhi" tree until he became "awakened." During a full moon, with the rising of the morning star, Siddhartha Gautama became the Buddha, the "awakened one," one who has realized the true nature of reality.

Although reluctant at first to teach what he had realized, Buddha went on to teach for forty-five years. His initial teaching focused on his insight regarding the cause of suffering and the path to be followed to eliminate suffering. These insights are known as the Four Noble Truths, which translate to:

1. Each life has some aspect of suffering or unsatisfactoriness;
2. The reason we experience suffering comes from our mind through our attachments, anger, and ignorance;
3. Suffering can be eliminated; and
4. Following the Eightfold Noble Path (a list of correct attitudes and actions) can eliminate suffering.

Ultimately Buddha concluded that suffering was a result of our delusions and ignorance about life, which orient us to engage in actions that cause harm to ourselves and others. As long as we remain ignorant to the true reality of life, that everything is impermanent, we continue to crave things to make us happy, which results in continued unhappiness and circumvents emotional well-being. His teachings were designed to help people awaken to the true nature of the world.

The Mindful Way: Attachments

- Close your eyes. Begin mindful breathing. Be aware of breathing in and breathing out—just rest your awareness there.
- Now let your mind fill with your attachments.
- *Recognize* the ideas and possessions to which you are attached. Recognize the people in your life to whom you are attached for external validation. *Accept* these attachments.

- *Investigate* these attachments. What do they represent? When and why were they developed? What emotions are attached to them? How does it *feel,* and where in the body do you feel it?
- *Non-identify* with these attachments. Say to yourself, "These are simply my attachments. They are not who I am."
- Just be with your attachments.
- Now imagine if you let go of, or loosened, some of these attachments.
- How does it feel in your body?
- How does the process of letting go of or loosening these attachments affect your energy?
- Let yourself simply feel the experience. And when you are ready, simply open your eyes.

After a time, you may want to write about this experience. Perhaps creating a list of your attachments will help you increase your awareness of them and allow you to be mindful of them. Remember, being mindful means not judging your experience and not judging your attachments.

Chapter Four

May the Force Be
With You: Constructs

"May the Force be with you." With these words, the film *Star Wars* captured the essence of many of the world's spiritual philosophies, particularly Eastern philosophies. What is the Force, and why should we want it to be with us? How can the Force help us, and how do we connect with it? Whether "the Force" is simply metaphorical or real, the answers to these questions can be both enlightening and meaningful.

"The Force" is a universal energetic field. It exists in all things. It exists everywhere. It is pure energy and is the cornerstone of the universe. It has always been and it will always be. It is like a river of energy that continuously flows, is always in motion, and carries with it the knowledge of the universe. It is as if we took Carl Jung's concept of the "collective unconscious," the part of our psyche that contains universal archetypes that we all inherit, and merged it with all the tiny little subatomic particles of the universe. This joining would create a stream of energy that contained the knowledge of everything that ever existed. Some have described the "soul," or "our spirit," as containing the same ingredients.

Why we would want to tap in to this source of energy should be obvious. Imagine connecting to a stream of energy that could enlighten you. Isn't that what enlightenment is all about? Isn't enlightenment aligning the self with the pure spirit of the universe, creating vast awareness and unlimited potential? Wouldn't it be wonderful if we could simply tap in to the Force at will and use it to benefit our existence? Well, maybe there is a way. Perhaps through our intuitive self we can summon the Force.

So how did they connect to the Force in *Star Wars*? Luke Skywalker's journey, as the young developing Jedi, provides some insight that can help us answer this question. As you may recall, Skywalker has the internal fortitude of a Jedi (as do we all), and the Jedi are able, at will, to connect to the Force and use it to their advantage. However, Skywalker is untrained in the art of summoning the Force. He is undisciplined, impulsive, unfocused, and annoyingly whiny.

Eventually Skywalker seeks out the Jedi Master Yoda, for it is Yoda who can train Skywalker in the art of the Jedi mind. Skywalker travels to a far-off planet in search of Yoda. Upon arrival, he stumbles upon a funny-looking creature living in a swamp. This creature is small in stature ("size matters not") and green in coloration, with long, pointed ears. He also talks with a funny lilt. Skywalker, consistent with his naiveté and impudent behavior, quickly dismisses this creature as one having little significance. Through a series of mishaps and an increase in Skywalker's frustration level, it is finally revealed to Skywalker that this funny little creature is in fact the Jedi Master Yoda.

Let's take a moment and analyze the significance of this plot line. Why not simply have Skywalker fly off to another planet and meet up with Master Yoda without all this chicanery? What benefit is it to Skywalker to go through all of these shenanigans? The benefit to him is rather significant. Skywalker had a preconceived notion of what a Jedi master would look like, how a Jedi master would behave, and how he would feel in the presence of such a master. He had built up a construct in his mind regarding how this whole process would likely unfold, and ultimately what the stature and status of a Jedi master would be. He was attached to this construct, which was based on his own projections of the world. He assigned certain attributes to what a Jedi master would look like and how a Jedi master would behave based on his own belief system, which was his own creation. This gives the viewer a small but significant snapshot into the mind of Skywalker.

As it turns out, Skywalker is rather conventional in his thinking. He has assigned attributes to the concept of Jedi master that are conventional in nature. One can infer from his initial reaction to Yoda that he expected (that is to say, he had a set of expectations) that Yoda would be the archetypal warrior. The archetypal warrior is masculine and bold. He is tall and muscular and, as a master, would be bright and articulate. He certainly would not be a funny little creature with green pointed ears. Skywalker's construct of a Jedi master was not only an illusion and quite delusional, it certainly didn't live up to reality. Of course, that is what we all do much of the time. We create constructs of how things ought to be. We develop expectations that are often not met. As our young man Skywalker did, we often overlook opportunity, despite the fact that it is right there in front of us.

Skywalker, as part of his Jedi training, needed to learn this lesson. He needed to embrace the age-old adage, "Don't judge a book by its cover." He further needed to challenge his constructs of the world. In order to be able to "feel the Force" and become a Jedi, Skywalker needed to change his worldview. He needed to expand his mind, increasing his concentration and awareness, while also letting go of his preconceptions. He needed to be more focused on his intuitive side and no longer allow his thoughts to dominate his experience.

Once Skywalker accepts Yoda as his teacher, his real training begins. Yoda directs Skywalker through a series of disciplined activities that are designed to increase Skywalker's ability to focus and concentrate. He schools him in the art of quieting the mind and focusing his attention and energy. "Concentrate," Yoda chides Skywalker. Eventually this process begins to bear fruit. Skywalker is able to close his eyes, shut out the interference of his mind, and concentrate with such single-mindedness that he is able to "feel the Force." Over time, as his concentration becomes more focused, he is able to access the Force with less and less effort. Hence, George Lucas, through his masterpiece film series *Star Wars*, demonstrates to the world the art and benefits of mindfulness and meditation.

Constructs

I have referred to the concept of "constructs," but I haven't given this concept the weight it merits or fully illustrated the impact constructs have on our emotional life.

A construct is essentially a psychological framework to which we attach ideas, images, and values about a particular thing or a set of things, in order to help us emotionally navigate the world. Often constructs contain the rules by which we live and the goals to which we aspire.

Freud's Constructs

Constructs can be so powerful that we forget that they are simply a concept, an idea. Freud, considered by many as the father of psychology, developed such powerful constructs that they became part of our culture and part of our everyday language. For example, let's examine his construct of the ego. In our culture, the term "ego" is used frequently. It's referred to so often that most of us forget that it is only a construct, and we relate to it as if it was a real thing, which it is not. Not only that, but how we use and understand the construct is very different from Freud's original construct. This is not an uncommon practice. Constructs often morph into other meanings than the original meaning they held. This process occurs over time and is influenced by culture and by context.

Let's take a moment to explore the meaning and the configuration of the original construct of "ego" and contrast it with our current common use. Freud developed three constructs of the mind: the "id," the "ego," and the "super-ego." These three constructs became the foundation for Freud's theories. The id represents our primitive nature, our instinctual needs, our impulses, and our drives. The id is driven to seek pleasure (Freud's pleasure principle) and avoid pain. It is wholly unconscious and does not reside in the real world. Freud described the id as "a cauldron full of seething excitations."[13] The problem is that the id needs immediate gratification, which can be difficult to obtain on an ongoing basis. When the id wants a breast, it wants it now. The breast doesn't even have to be real; it can be imagined. But if the baby is hungry, an imagined breast is simply not going to do the trick. The inability to gratify the id when it wants to be gratified leads to tension and frustration (anxiety).

Along comes the ego (as described by Freud) to help the id. According to Freud, "The ego represents what may be called reason and common sense, in contrast to the id, which contains the passions…"[14] The ego is designed to comprehend reality; it is a reality-based structure of the mind. Its task is to help satisfy the id's desires. It accomplishes this by learning all that it can about the real world and, in so doing, bringing real objects to satisfy the id. No longer will the id only have to imagine a breast; with the ego's help, it can have a real breast.

But can the infant, driven by the id and guided in reality by the ego, simply have any breast? Not in our world. Only certain breasts will do. So Freud developed another construct called the super-ego. The super-ego scans reality and chooses objects that are socially acceptable for the ego to bring to the id. It is the super-ego's job to locate an appropriate breast, one sanctioned by culture, society, and conscience as acceptable. The super-ego contains our sense of right and wrong and influences our behavior through guilt.

There you have it: the trinity of the mind. All three are nothing more than constructs. They are ideas about the mind, about our psyche. We cannot cut open our brain and take out the id, the ego, or the super-ego. Yet we often operate as if they are real, as if they really exist. They don't. They are organizing principles. They allow us to think about our mind in a certain way, but that's it. These constructs may be as farfetched as the construct that the world is flat or that the earth is the center of the universe.

The word "ego" is used in common vernacular to indicate something about a person's character. It often refers to our sense of self and, more specifically, our sense of self-importance or our self-pride or conceit. "He has a big ego" is intended to mean that he is "full of himself." It is often used in a pejorative manner.

The Self as a Construct (You're Not Always Who You Think You Are)

When you think or speak about yourself, when you say, "I," what you usually refer to is "me and my story." This is the "I" of your likes and dislikes, fears and desires, the "I" that is never satisfied for long. It is a mind-made sense of who you are, conditioned by the past and seeking to find its fulfillment in the future.

Eckhart Tolle, *Stillness Speaks*[15]

It may be confusing to think of the "self" as a construct, but in fact, that is what it actually is. We define our self using multiple constructs. We identify with our gender, race, ethnicity, age, marital status, likes and dislikes, etc. The list goes on and on. All of these are construct based.

Eastern philosophy challenges the very existence of the self. In his book *After the Ecstasy, the Laundry*, Jack Kornfield writes,

The emptiness of self shows itself in our lack of control over our supposedly fixed "self." Anyone who turns inward to meditation or prayer immediately encounters the ever-changing thought stream of the mind, and the endless ripples of moods and emotions that color each moment. These thought streams and emotions have a life of their own. In them a whole vision of our childhood or the replay of complex adult experiences appears, compels our attention, and disappears in moments. We usually take ourselves to be the sum of these thoughts, ideas, emotions, and body sensations, but there is nothing solid to hold them. How can we claim to be our thoughts or opinions or emotions or body when they never stay the same?[16]

Even if we challenge the premise that the self is simply a construct, and we hold firm that the self concretely exists and we know who we are, there can be surprising revelations. Often who we think we are may be very different than who we actually are. Furthermore, how we perceive reality may be different than what actually exists in reality.

Much of what we know about human emotion and psychology comes from decades of research. Research in the area of human subjects is tightly controlled, and specific standards must be met before research findings are considered valid. One challenge that many researchers face is how we can measure human behavior and human emotion from an objective rather than subjective position. Without going into too much detail regarding research protocol, the object is to have the research subject respond from an unbiased place. That is to say that the subject's responses are not consciously influenced by personal feelings, interpretations, or prejudice. This often translates to the need for the research to be crafty, to somehow disguise what the researchers are actually trying to measure.

Let's look at a few examples of research that were designed to determine if who we think we are is accurate and how these findings might affect human behavior and emotions. The following research studies looked at "prejudice" and "gender bias," a form of prejudice.

Malcolm Gladwell, in his book *Blink*, presents an interesting viewpoint regarding what is called the "adaptive unconscious."[17] Like

Freud's unconscious, the adaptive unconscious is a part of our mind that we are not aware of. However, this is not Freud's construct of instinctual drives. The role of the adaptive unconscious is to influence our judgments, behaviors, and feelings, and helps us categorize our world and generate intuitions. It is shaped by our experience of the world.

When given a test called the Implicit Association Test, a test designed to detect unconscious biases and the strength of a person's automatic associations, people who consciously believed that they are not prejudiced demonstrated prejudices. These prejudices, which reside in the unconscious, have been formed through associations. This process is similar to training our dog to sit. The dog associates the voice command "to sit" with praise, and perhaps a treat, and therefore sits. Our prejudices are associated with judgments we have learned through our world experience and are associated with that which we are prejudiced towards. These findings once again challenge how well we really know ourselves.

Gender bias is a form of prejudice. It is often unconscious and occurs when a person has a belief or an attitude that a gender is somehow inferior or simply less valuable. Gender bias means that an individual has a tendency to think about or behave toward people on the basis of gender. This suggests that a gender-biased person maintains some level of prejudice towards a specific gender. Often what we see, or what we believe to be the case, is that it is more likely for males to be gender biased towards females. Simply put, these males value males more highly than they value females. Certainly there is substantial evidence that this type of gender bias exists throughout the world. When this type of gender bias exists in a relationship between a man and a woman, the woman may often feel that her partner values her less than he values himself. This process can lead to real conflict. The woman may feel that she's never listened to, or feel that her views or opinions are not respected. These feelings can be hurtful. She may respond in anger, or she may simply withdraw from her partner. Her partner usually responds by defending himself and denies that he treats her in that manner. And around and around they go.

But what happens when the woman is also gender biased? What might even be a more intriguing question is, what happens when the woman is gender biased towards women?

In his book *The Social Animal*, Elliot Aronson cites a study conducted in the late sixties by Goldberg, and then replicated in 1983, that found some interesting data related to this issue. The study asks a group of college women to read and evaluate some scholarly articles. Some of the articles were assigned a male author's name, while the remainder of the articles were given a female author's name. The women were instructed to rate the value of these articles based on competency and style. Consistently, the articles containing a male author's name were rated higher than the articles containing a female author's name. These studies demonstrated that these women were gender biased against their own gender and viewed women as being inferior to men. And, of course, these women were unaware that gender bias was even being evaluated.[18]

Fortunately things have changed since these studies were conducted, but that doesn't mean that we don't carry around within our psyche some conditioned beliefs regarding our value and the value of others. The more our own value is dependent on how we perceive others perceiving us, the less secure we are and the more prone to anxiety we become.

Gender bias, or bias in general, is often a result of how we have been impacted by our environment, particularly when we were young and impressionable. We don't have to come from a home life that openly demonstrated prejudice. The process of developing gender bias can be the result of ongoing overt behavior on the part of an influential family member, someone who openly displays and reinforces bias. However, it is just as likely to develop on a covert level and then is incorporated into our psychological makeup. "Covert" simply suggests that the bias is not obvious. The child may observe a behavior (for example, the rolling of the eyes), or just "feel" the disapproving, condescending attitude of the biased individual.

In most social groups, including our home environment, there are different degrees of status assigned to the members of the group. When we discuss status in this context, we are discussing value. In many conventional family systems, and certainly in family systems of the past, men (father, son, grandfather) were given higher status than the rest of the family members. Much of this status was observable. That is to say that a child observed how members of the family behaved towards one another and could "sense" who the high-status holders were. The significance of this dynamic is that the attitudes held by the high-status holders were the attitudes that the young would often develop. If this attitude included bias, it was likely that the bias would be passed on to the child. Even in the case of young female family members who observed that the men were held in higher esteem (had high status), these youngsters grew up to be gender biased against women. The good news is, when we are mindful of our thoughts, feelings, and attitudes, we can change them.

Perhaps we don't know ourselves as well as we think we do.

The Construct of Marriage

Let's look at marriage as a construct. The definition of marriage often begins with "a social institution." If we look up the word "institution," in this context, we find the following description: "Institution, a well-established and structured pattern of behavior or of relationships that is accepted as a fundamental part of a culture, as marriage." (I found it humorous that just before this definition appears, we find this description: "Institution, a public or private place for the care or confinement of inmates, esp. mental patients.") So, is it a structured pattern of behavior or the confinement of inmates?

Marriage is a legal contract; however, it's also a construct: a set of ideas strung together to give us a sense of order, clarity, and security.

Marriage is something we aspire to. It is held in such high esteem in our culture that not to marry is often viewed as a negative. It wasn't too long ago that a young girl's ultimate dream was to marry, and if she did not, she failed to live up to life's expectations.

But the construct of marriage is just that: a construct. It is not that there is anything wrong with the construct; however, the construct often overrides the fundamental aspect of marriage, which is the connectedness and quality of the couple relationship. The construct of marriage emphasizes all sorts of beliefs about marriage that often overshadow the essence of the relationship. This may seem apparent, but it's not. People have strong attachments and fantasies about their ideas about marriage. When they are not met, disappointment and sometimes disaster befalls them. Moving beyond the construct and concentrating on the quality and the substance of the relationship is what is essential.

So often I have heard the following statement: "I thought once we were married, everything would be alright." This statement seems to presuppose that the construct of marriage has magical properties. Marriage rarely solves a relational problem, just like having a child rarely solves a marital problem. And yet we are governed by these constructs.

We need to be mindful of our constructs. We need to be aware of how our constructs shape our expectations and often lead us astray from the true nature of the experience. Imagine if Luke Skywalker never realized that Yoda was a Jedi master. What a missed opportunity for growth that would have been. How many missed opportunities have we all endured because of our constructs and expectations?

The Mindful Way: Constructs and Bias

- Close your eyes. Begin mindful breathing. Be aware of breathing in and breathing out— just rest your awareness there.
- Now shift your awareness to the constructs and biases in your life. Based on these constructs what are your beliefs? How have any of these constructs manifested in bias?

- Just be with this awareness. Accept what emerges. Do not judge it.
- Imagine what it might be like if you let go of some of these constructs.
- How does it feel in your body? Let yourself feel the experience.
- When you are ready, simply open your eyes.

Chapter Five

The War is Over?: Context

The year was 1974. World War II had been over for nearly thirty years, and yet 2nd Lt. Hiroo Onoda, a World War II soldier in the Japanese army, received a hero's welcome from his native Japan. Here is his story.

In 1942, Hiroo Onoda, age thirty, was drafted into the Japanese army. He was trained as an intelligence officer in guerilla warfare and, in 1944, was sent to Lubang Island, seventy-five miles southwest of Manila, Philippines. His commanding officer gave Onada the simple instructions, "Never surrender," and "Use any means necessary to hamper the operations of the enemy."

Eventually, Onoda moved deep into the mountains, outmaneuvering his enemy at every turn. Despite seeing surrender leaflets dropped by airplanes, declaring that the war was over, he was convinced that these were simply part of the American propaganda machine and continued his service as a Japanese officer.

In 1974, Norio Suzuki, a Japanese university student, decided to leave the university and travel the world in search of Lt. Onoda. He was successful. He found and befriended Lt. Onoda. He tried to convince Onoda that the war was over and he should return home to Japan. But Onoda, committed to his original orders, said that he would never surrender unless instructed to do so by his superior officer.

Suzuki returned to Japan to tell his story and shortly thereafter returned to the island with Major Taniguchi, one of Onoda's superior officers. Major Taniguchi commended Lt. Onoda for his excellent and dedicated service to the Japanese army and then ordered Onoda to lay down his arms and surrender.

With his well-conditioned .25 caliber rifle, five-hundred rounds of ammunition, and several grenades, 2nd Lt. Hiroo Onoda emerged from the Philippine jungle to surrender, twenty-nine years after Japan's formal surrender, and fifteen years after he had been declared dead by the Japanese army.

Context

Every behavior must be viewed within the context in which it takes place.

How can we understand why Lt. Onoda continued his service for decades, believing he was still at war, despite evidence to the contrary? The explanation is simple: context. His experience and behavior was based on the context in which he lived. He *believed* that the war was still going on. He was told never to surrender, and until a superior commanding officer reversed these orders, he would continue operating within this context.

Interestingly, throughout the many years that Lt. Onoda maintained his role as a Japanese officer, he had several encounters with the police and inhabitants of the island. Some of these encounters resulted in gunfire, bloodshed, and even death. However, upon his surrender, the

Philippine government took into consideration the "context" of his behavior, and President Ferdinand Marcos gave Onoda a full pardon.

A Client's Context

Some time ago, I had a client call me in the morning, requesting an emergency session. She told me that she was feeling very unnerved, highly anxious, and rather impulsive, and needed to see me so she didn't "do something stupid." I arranged to have a session with her as quickly as I could, with the agreement that she would not do anything detrimental to her well-being.

The client arrived for her session, and it was apparent that she was in a very agitated state. Prior to inquiring about what had caused this response, I asked her to sit for awhile, eyes closed, and simply concentrate on her breathing. She began to calm. Eventually, I asked her to open her eyes and tell me what had occurred.

In a rather calm voice, she told me the following story: "When I got to work this morning, I was walking down the hall, and my boss passed by and didn't say 'good morning.'"

"And?" I said. At this point she began to become a little more agitated. I instructed her to return to her breathing and calm herself down. When she became calm, she continued her story. She said, "I know he hates me and I know he wants to fire me, so I'm just going to quit. I was going to quit right before I called you, but you talked me out of it."

"Hasn't he always given you good evaluations? What makes you think he hates you and is going to fire you?" I inquired.

"Well," she said, "what kind of person doesn't say 'good morning' to you unless they hate you and want to get rid of you?"

What should be obvious from this story is the perspective from which my client experienced this encounter, which was, "If my boss doesn't say good morning to me, then it means that he hates me and is going to fire me." She was obviously attached to the "good morning" interaction and what it signified to her. When she didn't receive it, she crumbled. No other possibilities entered her mind. She hadn't considered her boss at all. She hadn't had the presence of mind to even imagine that he might be preoccupied in thought or deed, or simply in a bad mood.

What may have fueled this perspective? The answer is the context in which she experienced this encounter. Her mind (the context) was attached to the meaning of a morning greeting, and when it was not received, she suffered. But there is more to this story than meets the eye. Why was she so attached? Why wasn't her mind in a state of nonattachment? She was in a state of attachment because she was generally filled with anxiety and, as a result, looked to the outside world to validate her and give her a sense of well-being. The mind has to be calm in order to be nonattached, and we have to be nonattached in order for our mind to be calm.

Consider the relationship that most pet owners have with their pets. I have had many clients that have very powerful, loving relationships with their pets, while maintaining less-than-fulfilling relationships with their family members. Why should this be the case? Doesn't the fact that they can maintain a loving relationship with another living thing indicate that they are capable of loving? I would argue that it does. Then what gets in the way in their personal relationships? Attachment!

What's interesting about relating to a pet is that our context is different. Many of us are extremely attached to our pets, but not primarily because they validate us. Our attachment is more of a healthy attachment. If anything, our pets often serve as a source for us to share our love. The context in which we experience our pets is much more reflective of nonattachment. This is not to say that we aren't validated by the love our pets give us. This is to suggest that on the level in which our mind perceives this relationship, we are less guarded and less anxious about the harm our pets could do to us. Even when our pets act in injurious ways, we are quick to dismiss their behavior. How might you react if your spouse peed on your favorite chair? Once again, this is an example of nonattached engagement, in which the nonattached context in which we experience our pets allows us to more fully engage.

Imagine the following circumstance:

> He entered the building, gun in hand, and shot the man in the chest and killed him.

What are your initial thoughts? Because someone just shot and killed somebody, you will most likely interpret this event negatively. However, if I simply change the context and tell you that the man entering the building is a police officer, engaged in a rather heroic mission to save dozens of people being held hostage by a lunatic gunman who has already killed three people, you are likely to interpret this event completely differently.

Every behavior must be viewed within the context in which it takes place. The context, however, is your mind. When I offered additional information about the event, your mind simply interpreted the event from a different perspective.

Brooklyn, NY

Years ago, when I was a freshman in college in Brooklyn, NY, I got ripped off for fifty dollars, which at that time was a considerable amount of money. I was a young student, with very little money, and passionate about music. I was at a stage where I really wanted my own stereo equipment. However, stereo equipment was very expensive.

One day I walked into the student lounge and saw a friend of mine engaged in conversation with one of his friends. I joined the conversation, which happened to be about music and stereo equipment (we talked about this a lot). After several minutes, a bell rang in the background, announcing that the next class period was beginning. My friend said his goodbyes and off to class he went, leaving me alone in the conversation. I said, "I really want to buy an amp, but they are so expensive and I don't have much money." My friend's friend said, "I could get you a great deal on a practically new amp that my friend is selling for fifty bucks." He told me what type of amp it was, which I recognized to be of good quality. I was really excited about this and told him that I didn't have the money on me, but if he was willing to wait, I could get it and be back here in a half an hour. He said, "Sure," but I had better hurry back because he had class during the next period.

I raced off and borrowed the money from my father, who happened to work only a couple of blocks away. My dad was cool about lending me the money, asked no questions, and knew that I would pay him back when I got home. I returned to the student lounge and gave the money to my friend's friend. He told me to wait in the student lounge and that he would be back in fifteen minutes with the amp. I said, "Cool." Fifteen minutes came and went, as did my fifty dollars. I waited for an hour and a half, hoping against hope that I hadn't been ripped off, which of course I had.

I felt so foolish. How could a "street-smart" New Yorker like myself get ripped off so easily? The answer is illuminated by the context in which I viewed this situation.

The next day I saw my friend and told him what occurred. I asked him about his friend and where I could find him to settle this matter. My friend informed me that "this guy" wasn't a friend of his. In fact, he told me, he had never seen him before. "But you were talking to him as if he was your friend," I said. "I was just being friendly," he replied. It's true that my friend made no formal introductions between me and "this guy," but that wasn't uncommon. I had assumed that they were friends, and any friend of a friend of mine is trustworthy.

The Mind as Context

My mind created a context in which I experienced this entire encounter. However, the context was simply false. My mind assumed that this stranger was a friend of a friend and therefore trustworthy. Had I known that this was a total stranger, I never would have given him fifty dollars and let him walk out of my sight. This is the power of context, and your mind is the creator of context.

The general definition of context is "the set of circumstances or facts that surround a particular event, situation, etc." or "the interrelated conditions in which something exists or occurs." A more specific understanding of context is the "landscape" in which the mind interprets perceptions and stimuli.

The mind serves as the background to our experiences. It's as if the mind is a canvas and our sense organs (sight, hearing, smell, touch, and taste) are like the brushstrokes of color. The makeup of the canvas (its texture, coloration, size, etc.) will affect how the medium placed onto the canvas will be experienced. Based on a host of factors, such as culture, ethnicity, gender, family attitudes, societal attitudes, physiological influences, prior events, and experiences, the context of our mind is shaped. And based on the influences of these factors at any given moment, the mind's context is always changing. For example, we experience things differently when we are calm and well rested than when we are tired and irritable.

Through the practice of mindfulness, the mind as context can be altered. Mindfulness orients us to the present moment. It enhances our awareness of the present moment and allows us to experience life in a fresh and less-encumbered way. In his book *The Mindful Brain,* Dr. Dan Siegel, a professor and neuroscientist, refers to this present-moment awareness as a "bottom-up" experience. A bottom-up experience is "raw, in-the-moment sensory data that emerges into awareness."[19] It is not influenced by prior learning. A "top-down" experience is influenced by our past. For example, if we as adults were to smell a rose, all of our prior learning about roses would come into play and significantly influence how we experience that rose in the present moment. Siegel believes that mindfulness cultivates the ability to get back to bottom-up experiences, resulting in a life with wonder and curiosity, as if seeing something for the first time.

In this way, our mind context is more representative of what has been called the "beginner's mind." Beginner's mind, a term used by Zen Master Suzuki Roshi, refers to having an attitude of openness, eagerness, and lack of preconceptions. It is the mind that is innocent of preconceptions and expectations, judgments and prejudices. Beginner's mind is just present to explore and observe and see things as they are.

In the beginner's mind there are many possibilities, but in the expert's there are few.

Suzuki Roshi, *Zen Mind, Beginner's Mind*[20]

The Mindful Way: Worldview

There is no greater context in which we experience our life than our worldview. The term "worldview" has been defined as "the overall perspective from which one sees and interprets the world. A collection of beliefs about life and the universe held by an individual or a group." Worldview refers to the framework of ideas and beliefs through which an individual interprets the world and interacts with it.

- Close your eyes. Begin mindful breathing. Be aware of breathing in and breathing out—just rest your awareness there.
- Now shift your awareness to your worldview. What is your view of the world? Is the world a joyous, safe place, or a hostile, unsafe place? How do you consider the nature of most people? Are you generally open to people, or are you cautious about people? How open or rigid are your beliefs? Is your view more reflective of a "glass half empty" or a "glass half full"?

- Just sit with your worldview.
- Imagine how your worldview affects how you perceive things and how you experience things. Imagine how a minor shift in your worldview could change the way you might experience the world.
- Let yourself simply feel the experience. And when you are ready, simply open your eyes.

The next time you find yourself reacting to a situation, be mindful of the context in which you are experiencing it. Ask yourself, "What is the context in which I'm having this experience? Am I tired? Am I frightened? Is there another way to view this situation?" Let your mind consider other possibilities.

Chapter Six

The Dream Tribe:
Scarcity and Abundance

In a faraway land, there once lived a tribe known as the "dream tribe." Each morning the tribe would gather in several groups and begin the day by discussing their prior night's dreams. And each evening they would gather in groups and discuss what they intended to dream that night. They were essentially a lucid-dreaming community, one that had practiced this dream ritual since the beginning of time. They were an agrarian community, and farming and dreaming was their life. They lived in harmony with their environment and, as with most farmers, were very aware of the seasons. They knew what season was best to plant and what season was best to harvest. They were a peaceful, contented people.

One year, the seasons did not unfold in a typical manner. The heat of summer never seemed to abate and the rains never came. As a result, the tribe lost most of their crop and, with it, their main food source. This pattern continued for a long time until the tribe was entrenched in a terrible famine. Their very existence was at risk.

The elders of the tribe spent many hours discussing the situation in an attempt to find a solution to this horrible problem. During one such meeting, it became evident to the community that discussions were not going well. In a rare display of anger and frustration, the elders were shouting at one another. A large crowd gathered around the elders to listen to what was being said.

During the time of what would become known as the "Great Debate," the women of the tribe, as was their custom, were preparing the evening meal. Their food stock was very low. They approached the gathering, carrying their baskets of food, and sat to listen to the elder's arguments.

"We should feed only the elders, for they carry the wisdom of the tribe," one member of the council argued.

"No, no, no. We should feed the warriors, because it is their strength that protects the tribe from outside invasion," another said. Yet another said, "We should feed the children for they are our future."

Each orator was adamant about their position. Soon the shouting intensified, and it looked as though the council would begin to fight.

During this commotion, one of the women reached into her basket and started to distribute the food among the gathering. No one dared eat, not without guidance from the elders. Finally she lifted her plate, took a handful of food, and fed it to the person sitting nearest to her. The crowd looked on in amazement until a second woman lifted her plate, took a handful of food, and fed it to the person sitting next to her. Before long, the entire tribe was feeding the person sitting next to them.

From that moment on, each morning, mid-day, and evening meal was practiced in this manner. Soon the famine passed.

Years later, as the woman who began what was to be called "the feeding ritual" lay on her deathbed, she was asked by a few of the young women what had inspired her to do what she did that evening. With tears in her eyes, this old, frail, wise being said, "The night before the elder's council, I had a dream. In the dream, we the People were sitting in a large circle, arms linked together, swaying back and forth.

We were all interconnected." She paused for a moment to reflect, and then continued and said, "As the screams and arguments of the men were ringing in my ears, I looked across from me and saw this thin young woman. She seemed terrified. My heart went out to her, and all I wanted to do was comfort her. Without even thinking about what I was doing, my hand reached down to my meager plate of food and scooped up some rice. As I offered my hand of rice to her lips, I was filled with love for her and wanted to give her the most precious gift I had: my food. Before long, all were doing exactly what I had done. All were giving."

Scarcity versus Abundance

The story of the "dream tribe" certainly illustrates the meaning of scarcity, and in fact, one definition of the term "scarcity" is famine. But this story also characterizes the concept of *abundance,* a term that means "a great amount of."

From an emotional point of view, it is interesting to observe and evaluate whether a person or a culture operates from a position of scarcity or abundance. Either position can significantly influence our mind context. When we operate from a context of scarcity, there never seems to be enough, regardless how much there actually is. When we operate from a context of abundance, there always seems to be enough, regardless of how little there is. These are powerful determinants of how we interpret our world, how we act in the world, and our overall emotional functioning. The purpose of addressing the concepts of scarcity and abundance is not to focus on the concrete meaning of these terms, but rather to view these terms within the context of emotionality.

Emotional Scarcity

Scarcity, from an emotional vantage point, is a "less than" model. This model is indicative of someone who believes or behaves as though there is not enough. It doesn't actually matter what there is not enough of, or even if there is actually not enough. What matters is that on a psychological level, this person's demeanor will be significantly influenced by an internal experience that resources are limited, that love and goodwill is limited. Once we operate from this vantage point, we become protective of our resources, fearful that they will vanish, and we will defend against this likelihood. Our worldview is that there is not enough for everyone, and we better protect that which is ours. We operate from a place of protectiveness that ultimately engenders fear and anxiety, which in turn is an emotionally contracting experience. The fictional character Scrooge from Dickens' *A Christmas Carol* epitomizes this demeanor, what I call "emotional scarcity."

In contrast, when we operate from a place of abundance, we embrace the idea that there is plenty for all. This embrace creates a non-threatening, non-protective feeling within us. It allows us to be open, not defended, and therefore not fearful and filled with anxiety. It is an emotionally expansive experience and allows us to be giving. By nature, this posture is nonrestrictive. As Shakespeare said, "What's mine is yours and what's yours is mine." Mother Teresa of Calcutta epitomized operating from a place of abundance.

Let's look at the character Scrooge. Although his behavior indicates that he operates from a model of scarcity, such as hoarding and miserly behavior, it is his emotional stance in the world that truly gives his character meaning. Scrooge is a highly defended, emotionally closed, uncaring, anxious character. His overriding need is to protect himself emotionally. This need is based on the anticipation that others will take from him, leaving him in a vulnerable, weaker position. Therefore his manner is often hostile which distances him from others. He is so emotionally removed from society he cannot fully embrace the meaning of Christmas, and he is loath to allow his clerk, Bob Cratchit, time off to spend with his family.

As we can see from the Scrooge story, a key component of emotional scarcity is the defended nature of the individual. Let's look at how the popular TV series *Star Trek* illustrated this disposition. The starship Enterprise had a highly developed defense mechanism called "the shields," which were an invisible source of energy that would surround the entire ship. When the ship was under attack, it had the option to raise the shields. Captain Kirk would intercom Scotty (Mr. Scott, his chief engineering officer) and command, "Raise the shields." The shields would be raised, protecting the Enterprise from incoming fire. However, "the shields" were not invincible, and there were certain dynamics of this system that were restrictive. One such dynamic was that when the shields were up, protecting the ship from incoming fire, the Enterprise was unable to launch anything on an outgoing basis. This rendered the ship's weapon system virtually inoperable, so in effect, the Enterprise could not fight back.

In addition to restricting access to its weapons, maintaining the shields took an enormous amount of energy, and there was a finite amount of energy to be used for this purpose. Each time the shields "took a hit" from incoming fire, they would use additional energy to combat the impact, which resulted in lowering the available energy to maintain the shields. This meant that eventually the shields would falter, and the ship would be vulnerable to the attack. Although the shields could be a useful tool given the right circumstance, ultimately they were not the answer to an effective battle plan.

Like Scrooge, many people operate in the world from an emotionally restricted place, their shields in place. They are guarded and protective of their emotional space. These are not your warm, fuzzy types. They tend to operate from a rational perspective and feel very uneasy when confronted by emotions. They see the world through a linear lens and are more comfortable with facts and figures than they are with human interactions. They maintain an emotional system based on scarcity. And they are not alone.

Often their counterparts, the overly dramatic types, are also operating from a place of scarcity. Although they don't appear to be emotionally restricted, they are still driven by the fear that there isn't enough or they won't get enough. They become motivated to go out there and get all that they can before the other guy does. And once they have it, they will protect it and not let anyone close enough to take it away. These are the people who are envious and jealous when other people receive.

Either emotional posture, emotionally restrictive or overly dramatic, is a response to fear, which is a condition of unhealthy attachment and based on a context of scarcity.

Emotional Abundance

Embracing abundance is no easy task. It is difficult to give up a model that seems to have protected us and given us a sense (albeit false) of control in the world.

Consider the poor, orphaned child who has never experienced "enough" and who, at the age of ten, has the good fortune to be adopted by a moderately wealthy couple. Left by himself in the couple's dining room, he sees a bowl of fruit sitting on the table. Out of instinct, he quickly snatches as much fruit as he can carry and runs to his bedroom to stash his loot. He does this time and time again, until one day his adoptive father says to him in a rather casual manner, "You know, we will always fill that bowl with fruit." Eventually the boy learns to trust in his environment and stops hording the fruit.

In contrast, consider this story that characterizes a person operating from a place of emotional abundance.

The Wise Woman's Stone

A wise woman who was traveling in the mountains found a precious stone in a stream. The next day, she met another traveler who was hungry, and the wise woman opened her bag to share her food. The hungry traveler saw the precious stone and asked the woman to give it to him. She did so without hesitation. The traveler left, rejoicing in his good fortune. He knew the stone was worth enough to give him security for a lifetime.

A few days later the traveler came back to return the stone to the wise woman. "I've been thinking," he said, "I know how valuable the stone is, but I give it back in the hope that you can give me something even more precious. "What's that?" asked the wise woman. The traveler replied, "Give me what you have within you that enabled you to give me the stone."[21]

Emotional abundance is what enables us to be giving. It is an emotionally expansive experience and allows us to feel good about ourselves and world around us. Imagine what our world would be if only we embraced the model of abundance.

The Mindful Way: Abundance

- Close your eyes. Begin mindful breathing. Be aware of breathing in and breathing out—just rest your awareness there.
- Now imagine a world filled with abundance. What does this look like? How does this feel? Where do you feel it in your body?
- Let yourself simply experience these feelings. Rest in the awareness that the world is filled with abundance, as are you. When you are ready, simply open your eyes.

Be mindful about your reactions that appear to be based on scarcity. Bring your awareness to these responses. Do not judge yourself. Ask yourself, "Is there another way to respond? How would I respond if I were to operate from a place of abundance?"

Chapter Seven

From Russia with Love: Intention

Our intention creates our reality.

Dr. Wayne Dyer[22]

In 1984, I was asked to join a group of psychotherapists from North America to journey to the Soviet Union. The group, comprised of about thirty therapists, would spend about a month traveling to and through the Soviet Union, visiting mental health sites, psychological institutions, educational institutions of psychology, and any other organization related to the practice of psychology. We would fly to Finland and, after a few days of acclimating, travel by train to Leningrad (now called St. Petersburg) to begin our journey.

At that time this was a rather unusual journey, given the fact that the Soviet Union was under a Communist regime regarded as "unfriendly" to Americans. We were warned of the potential complications that could exist, as well as the restrictions under which we had to travel. However, my decision to make this journey was in fact an easy one. Regardless of the potential challenges, this trip was a culmination of an *intention* that was born early in my childhood. Interestingly, I didn't seek out this trip. In fact, I knew nothing about it until one day a fellow psychotherapist mentioned it to me and asked if I would be interested in joining this group.

Sometimes intentions manifest without us even being aware of the energy we hold towards our intention. The trip itself was not the manifestation of my intention. The manifestation of the intention is what occurred during the trip. I will explain.

In the late 1890s, my grandfather, when he was just seventeen, accompanied by his eighteen-year-old brother, boarded a steamship from Russia destined for the United States. It was the brothers' task to relocate to America and earn enough money to bring their entire family to America. The two boys set sail to America. They had very little money, knew no one on the opposite shore, were unable to speak the language, and, I imagine, felt a mixture of dread and hope in their hearts. America represented the land of opportunity. They would work hard so they could earn enough money for every member of the family to join them in their new world and new life.

For over sixty years, my grandfather worked as a hat maker on the lower east side of New York. He and his brother saved all of their money and periodically sent it back to Russia to provide passage for a sister, a brother, a cousin, and then finally, after many years, their mother and father.

This is not an uncommon story. This is the story of America. People relocating from all parts of the globe, seeking a better life, a life free from tyranny and oppression, a life based on the principles of freedom. My family was no exception.

So it is understandable why I might desire to visit Russia and somehow reconnect with my roots. However, my motivation felt deeper than this. My family name is "Kobrin," and as early as I can remember, I was told that we come from a small little village somewhere in Russia named Kobrin. But a debate seemed to surface at every major family gathering. Depending on the storyteller (usually an uncle), and depending on how much the uncle had to drink at the time, either the town Kobrin was named after our family (as told with great pride), or we took the name Kobrin from the town (as told by the more practical uncle). As a young child, listening intently to my uncles argue over the origin of my family name, I knew that someday I would locate Kobrin and visit this village. My intent was powerful.

So in 1984, as a result of being asked to join this group and travel to the Soviet Union, I committed to finding the location of Kobrin and visiting the town. Somehow I was determined to finally manifest my lifelong intention.

But this was no easy task. Kobrin was a tiny little town located somewhere in a huge country. There was no Internet to assist me. After considerable research I was able to locate the town, but it was in an area of the Soviet Union that was "off limits," "closed," to foreign travelers. I phoned the US Embassy, as well as the Soviet Union Embassy in Washington, DC, and told them my story. Neither was very interested. Both informed me that it was impossible to travel to this area of the Soviet Union. This information was indeed a setback, but it was not going to deter me from going on the trip or from continuing to pursue my intent to visit the town of Kobrin.

I departed San Francisco and eventually met with the entire group in Finland. After spending a couple of days in Finland, we boarded a train that would take us on a fairly long journey to Leningrad. At that time, travel through the Soviet Union required that foreign travelers be accompanied by a guide who was appointed by, and a member of, the Communist Party. Travelers were only allowed to stay at state-sponsored designated hotels known as Intourist hotels. Once we arrived in Leningrad, we were met by our "guide" and ushered to an Intourist hotel. A limited number of Intourist hotels existed throughout the country. This is where the story gets interesting.

During our official tour of Leningrad, I had an opportunity to discuss with our guide my desire to travel to the town of Kobrin. I asked her if she had ever heard of Kobrin and explained my connection to the town. She told me that she had never heard of such a town and had no knowledge of how I could travel there. I asked her if she might know anyone who might know something about the town and requested that she keep it in mind.

After spending nearly a week in Leningrad, the group flew to Georgia (a state in the USSR) to visit the town of Tbilisi. Given the distance to travel, our guide stayed behind and would reconvene with us a week later in Moscow. Once arriving in Tbilisi, we were assigned a new guide. I asked this guide about Kobrin as well, and her answer was the same as our other guide: she had no knowledge of the town. After about a week in Tbilisi, we flew to Moscow, where we would spend the remainder of our time in the Soviet Union.

Upon arriving in Moscow, we were met by our original guide, who had arranged transportation by bus to our next Intourist hotel. Before boarding the bus, the guide told me that she had something to tell me and asked if I would sit next to her during the ride to the hotel, which of course I did.

As we drove to the hotel, the guide said to me in a very enthusiastic manner, "You'll never guess what happened." She went on to explain that during her layover awaiting our return, she roomed with another official guide. She asked the guide if she had ever heard of a town named Kobrin. To her surprise, the guide answered, "Oh yes, I know everything there is to know about Kobrin." Our guide was flabbergasted and encouraged her roommate to tell her all she knew.

As it turned out, Kobrin was famous for one particular event in Russia's history. In 1795, during the Polish uprising against Imperial Russia, there was a military Russian general who distinguished himself during a decisive battle that took place near the town of Kobrin. As a result of his victory, which apparently was a turning point in the war, the general was awarded the highest Medal of Honor and was given a country estate. The estate was in the small countryside town of Kobrin. Eventually, after the death of the general, the estate was turned into a museum and still exists today.

The guide told me that the town of Kobrin was about a forty-five minute drive from the city of Brest in Belarus, USSR. Brest, which was about a twelve-hour train ride from Moscow, had an Intourist hotel. She explained that if I was able to obtain a visa to visit the city of Brest, then possibly I could obtain a second "day-long" visa to visit Kobrin. This had never been done before.

The guide and I sat and talked for a long time, trying to establish a plan that could result in my ability to obtain these visas. We finally decided that I had to petition the visa office in Moscow, requesting both visas, one for Brest and one for Kobrin, on the grounds that my family heritage was significantly linked to Kobrin. We concocted a story that my great-great-grandparents were servants of the famous general: my great-great grandmother his chamber maid, and my great-great grandfather his stable boy. They had fallen in love, married under the permission of the general, and took the name of the town, Kobrin, as their surname. I would say that it was my desire and right to visit the birthplace of my family's origin. The guide called the Moscow visa office and set up an appointment for me to make my appeal. The rest was up to me.

Early the next morning, I arrived at the visa office. It was a very official-looking state building, adorned with Communist flags and pictures of the Soviet president in each room. It was a very intimidating environment. I entered through the main hall and was directed to an area to sit and wait. They knew exactly who I was. I waited. Eventually, someone came and directed me to follow him to a small, dimly lit room. Seated in the room, behind an old wooden desk, was what appeared to be a highly decorated general in a uniform adorned with medals and ribbons. On either side of him were seated two stodgy-looking women, each with hair tied tightly in a bun, also wearing some type of uniform. I was seated directly in front of the general.

For some time nothing was said. The general sat staring across the table at me. Finally, one of the women, who spoke English, asked me to explain my request. Slowly, with as much confidence as I could muster, I began to tell my story. I told them that I had always known that my family originated from the town of Kobrin, and it was my lifelong intention to visit the estate where my great-great-grandparents served the great General Suvorov (I practiced pronouncing that name for hours). There, I explained, my great-great-grandparents met, fell in love, married, and took the name of Kobrin as their surname. I told them that I was the first of my family to return to Russia and carried the entire family's wishes to visit the roots of our family heritage. I expressed to them that it would be a great honor to be able to accomplish this goal and that, if they permitted me to do so, I would be forever indebted to their generosity. The woman ended the interview and requested me to leave. The general never said a word, nor did they tell me what would happen next. I got back to the Intourist hotel, found our guide, and told her what had occurred. She said, "Now you wait."

Late the next afternoon, I was contacted by an official of the Intourist hotel and told to return to the visa office at 9:00 a.m. the next morning, which is precisely what I did. This time I was greeted by a less-threatening-looking person, who accompanied me to a more pleasant-looking room (not that much more pleasant). Once again there was an old wooden table with a wooden chair positioned in front. Behind the table sat a non-uniformed, middle-aged woman with a rather pleasant demeanor. She motioned me to sit. She said, "Before we begin, there is something I would like to say. I have been working in this office for more than thirty years and I have never seen this occur before. In my hand I hold not one visa, but two visas: one two-day visa for Brest and one twelve-hour visa for Kobrin." She hesitated for a moment and then said, with a wry smile on her face, "You must have been born under a lucky star." She sat for a moment in reflection and then added, "Surely you must believe in God." Imagine a member of the Communist party saying such a thing:

"Surely you must believe in God." Whether it was God, intention, or both, I was on my way to Kobrin.

My train to Brest left at 6:00 p.m. that evening. It was a twelve-hour train ride, and I would travel overnight in a sleeping car. The entire group accompanied me to the train station to bid me farewell. However, this farewell was as much precautionary as it was to wish me well. There was tension in the group regarding my travel. Many of the group members were very apprehensive about me leaving the safety of the group to travel to unknown parts of the Soviet Union.

During our stay in Tbilisi, the group had suffered a trauma that had significantly influenced this attitude. One night, during our stay in Tbilisi, the KGB showed up at our Intourist hotel and demanded that one of the group members accompany them to KGB headquarters for questioning. As this young lady was being ushered out of the building by two KGB officers, our group leader, a veteran of Soviet Union travel, positioned himself between the hotel door and the KGB. "She's not going anywhere!" he shouted. An argument in Russian ensued that was quite heated. The entire group assembled to witness this encounter. Finally, after several minutes of yelling and screaming, the KGB surrendered the woman to the group leader and left in a huff. "Never," our group leader proclaimed, "willingly go anywhere with the KGB." He turned and left the group.

As it turned out, the KGB encounter was prompted by an event that I was party to in Leningrad. The aforementioned woman was a young psychotherapist from Philadelphia. She had been active in an organization that supported the rights of individuals in the Soviet Union who had been known as Refuseniks. Refuseniks were individuals, predominantly Soviet Jews, who had requested permission to leave the Soviet Union and emigrate to another country. When permission was denied, they became known as a Refusenik and were often stripped of their possessions, forced out of their homes, and forced to leave their jobs. Many of these individuals were highly educated and were thought of as the "Soviet brain trust." They were not allowed to leave for fear that their leaving could compromise Soviet security. Furthermore, by setting an example and stripping these individuals of their basic rights, the Soviet government hoped to deter further exit requests.

One day, during a time when there was nothing scheduled for the group, this woman asked me to accompany her to the home of a Refusenik. Although I may have known a little about Refuseniks, I really didn't know much about the fate of an individual deemed by the state to be a Refusenik. So with great curiosity, an eye for adventure, and compassion in my heart, we set off to find this individual.

Equipped with an address, we traveled by bus and train to unfamiliar parts of the city. We arrived at an old, dilapidated, walk-up apartment building. As we entered the building, a feral cat lunged by us, hissing his discontent at our arrival. We walked up seven flights of stairs and found the apartment we were looking for. Timidly we knocked at the door. A little, old, wrinkled-faced lady with a babushka on her head answered the door. She spoke no English, but somehow we were able to communicate our intentions. She gestured to us to come into the apartment.

It was a very tiny apartment, and it was evident that it had many inhabitants. We were approached by a man who appeared to be in his sixties, but it was hard to tell if he simply appeared to be older than he actually was. He spoke English. We had found our Refusenik. He asked us to sit in the parlor and he told us his story.

After providing us with tea, he told us that he had been the number-one nuclear physicist in all of the Soviet Union. However, after he had requested an exit visa to relocate to Israel, the government stripped him of everything, including his job. He was forced to move into his mother's apartment and share the space with several boarders. He told us that he had attempted to contact several highly placed US government officials, including Henry Kissinger, pleading for them to intercede with the Soviet government on his behalf. He then gave my companion a letter that apparently told his story, and she agreed to make sure that it would wind up in the hands of someone who would try and help him. We finished our tea, accompanied by large white sugar cubes, and then we left.

It was a very moving experience. Although I was alert to the possibility that we could be followed, there was no indication that we were, until Tbilisi.

The Tbilisi experience created significant paranoia within the group. And it was this paranoia that surrounded my departure to Kobrin. But I didn't feel paranoia or trepidation. This part of the journey was the fulfillment of a lifelong intention. I can't even explain why it was so important to me, but it was. Perhaps I simply needed to put to rest that age-old argument of whether the town was named after us or we were named after the town.

The train ride to Brest was uneventful. I arrived at the train station at about 6:00 a.m. in a scene that was reminiscent of a Hitchcock film. The smoke was rising from wheels of the train. The fog hovered about the train station, and the whole environment seemed to be in black and white. And as if that wasn't dramatic enough, I was approached by a man in a trench coat—that's right, a trench coat—who came up to me and said, "Follow me." No introduction; no handshake; just "Follow me," like he was Arnold Schwarzenegger from *Terminator 2:* "Follow me if you want to live."

I followed this man to a car that was waiting around the side of the building, engine running, driver smoking a cigarette. He opened the rear door and motioned to me to get in. He assumed the front passenger seat and off we went. We drove for about twenty minutes; not a word was spoken. We arrived at the Intourist hotel. He opened the rear door, ushered me out, and then drove off without a word.

The general manager of the hotel greeted me, and once again, I was told, "Follow me." He led me to the hotel registration desk and informed me that the clerk behind the counter would check my papers and register me. He then disappeared. After several minutes, during which time I was providing passport, visas, and any other form of identification required by the hotel clerk, the general manager reappeared from behind the registration counter. "Mr. Kobrin," he said, in fairly good English, "I'm afraid we have a problem. We will be unable to provide transportation for you to visit the town of Kobrin."

"What?" I said. "But it has been all arranged."

"Well, that is most unfortunate," he asserted. I stood there dumbfounded. I hadn't come all this way and gone through all that I had gone through to be denied now. Then it dawned on me. My New York brain kicked in. I reached into my pocket and pulled out a twenty-dollar bill. I reached out my hand and said, "Perhaps this could help you arrange some transportation." He took the twenty and said that I should be ready to depart in thirty minutes. I was led to my room, threw some water on my face, changed my clothes, and was ready to depart.

I returned to the lobby of the hotel, where I was greeted by yet another "tour guide." She spoke English and was a little younger than the previous guides I had encountered. She told me that the car that was to take me to the town of Kobrin was waiting outside, and if I would like, we could proceed immediately.

The drive to Kobrin was forty-five-minutes long through the countryside. The countryside was pleasant enough, but its features were still rather grayish and had an air of oppression. We arrived at the entrance to the town, where a beautiful large structure had the following Russian words inscribed on its surface: "Kobrin Founded 1292." I imagined that this sign, which I photographed many times, would put an end to the argument regarding our family name.

Later I discovered that the town had actually existed since the tenth century. I don't think my family was in Russia during the tenth century, but you never know. I was brought to the museum, the estate where my great-great-grandparents allegedly had met. The curator was delighted to meet me. He had never met a "Kobrin" before and told me that I was not only the first Kobrin to visit the town, but the first American. He treated me like I was royalty and insisted that he personally provide a tour of the museum.

After leaving the museum, I spent the rest of the day walking through the old town. I saw the destruction wrought upon the town during World War II. I was interested in seeing if any Jews still resided in Kobrin. There were very few. I had the pleasure of meeting one eighty-year-old man who told me the history of the plight of Kobrin's Jewish population. During World War II, the Germans invaded the town from Poland, just a short distance away, and rounded up the Jewish population and sent them to concentration camps. Very few ever returned. He told me that he was one of the lucky ones. He was able to be hidden during the invasion and stayed hidden until the end of the war, at which time he returned to the town. He pointed to an old stone building that had but one wall standing and said, "That is what's left of the synagogue." My guide and I moved on.

Later in the day we arrived at the newest addition to the town. Kobrin was once known as one of the finest woodcarving centers in Russia. In keeping with its heritage, the town opened a school in this area that specialized in woodcarving and furniture making. Once the school's director was made aware that a "Kobrin" from America was on the premises, he insisted on giving me a private tour of the facility. As we walked from room to room, he introduced me to all of his students. They were eager to meet me and shake my hand. Finally, the director presented me with two beautiful wood carvings, one hand carved and one made of beautiful, colorful mosaic wood chips. Both depicted the old mansion that the general had been given and was now the museum—and the mansion where my great-great-grandparents met, or so the story went.

As we departed Kobrin to drive back to the hotel, I reflected on the enormity of this experience. It was not only a meaningful and powerful day, but the mere fact that all of this was able to manifest was simply mind-blowing. For me, this experience was nothing short of miraculous, a miracle born out of a lifelong intention.

When I returned to the hotel, I was invited to "tea" with the hotel manager. This encounter turned out to be more of an interrogation than a friendly social call, with vodka served in addition to tea. The more the hotel manager drank, the more belligerent he became. He asked me to recall my every step during my visit to Kobrin, and report to him who I spoke with and what I said. As you might imagine, I grew increasingly uncomfortable in his presence. Finally, he brought up the recent incident in which the United States had accused the USSR of shooting down a Korean civilian airliner, killing 269 passengers off the eastern coast of Russia. I knew that I had to get out of there. I finally said the only thing I could think to say, which was, "If you hold on to your beliefs about the evils of the United States, and I hold onto the belief that USSR is an evil empire, then you and I can never be brothers, and that makes me sad." The words hung in the air for what seemed an eternity. Finally he waved his hand at me in a dismissive fashion and said, "You can go." That was the end of the interrogation.

That night I was called from my hotel room, under the ruse that someone was waiting to talk to me at the hotel bar. I left my room and went to the bar. No one was there to meet me. I decided to sit and wait to see if someone would show up. After about twenty minutes, I left the bar and returned to my room. When I returned to my room, it was apparent that someone had entered my room and gone through my things. It wasn't until I returned home that I realized that a canister of film had been taken. However, it did not contain my pictures of Kobrin.

I spent the next day mainly waiting for the train ride back to Moscow. My guide showed me some of the main sites of Brest, which included a very moving memorial dedicated to the Russian victims of World War II. Until that moment, I hadn't realized that Russia lost more than twenty million people during the war. My guide and I, seated upon a stone bench positioned in the middle of the memorial, reflected in silence until she timidly asked, "May I ask you something?"

"Of course," I said.

She continued, "I understand that in the United States there are people who do not have homes and sleep on park benches. Is this true?"

I paused for a moment, feeling somewhat embarrassed, before answering. "Not really. We have always had what we refer to as 'bums' who travel from place to place, but they represent a very small part of our population." I have never forgotten that conversation. My guide seemed to know more about the problem than I. This was consistent with my overall experience. The people of the USSR, and particularly the younger people, knew far more about the United States than we knew about the USSR.

That evening I boarded an overnight train back to Moscow. Shortly after the train left the station, there was a knock at my door. It was a Soviet officer, adorned in military uniform, with a bottle of vodka in one hand and two glasses in the other. "Comrade," he said, "please, join me in a drink." He walked into my berth, poured two glasses of vodka, handed me a glass, said "Skol," and downed the shot before I even had a chance to put lips to glass rim.

This visitor spoke very little English, but I was able to ascertain that he was stationed in East Germany and had very strong opinions about America. Once again, the more he drank, the more belligerent he became. Finally I excused myself, knocked at the door of the berth adjacent to mine, which I knew was being occupied by an African student who spoke English and Russian, and pleaded for his help. He came to my berth, and together, with some effort, managed to get the soldier to leave. I didn't sleep much that night.

I arrived in Moscow and rejoined my group, who was overjoyed to see me. After a few days we all boarded a train back to Finland. With the exception of some rather intense custom inspections, we all made it through without incident. It was a remarkable experience, one that I wanted to share in detail and at length because I believe it was born out of intention.

Intention

Intention rouses the mind and moves it along with all other concomitant factors towards an object. A classic example is that of iron filings and a magnet. Just as iron filings are helplessly drawn by a magnet, the mind helplessly engages an object due to the power of this mental factor intention.

Vajrayana Institute, Sydney, Australia[23]

Intention is a major component of mind context. It is both future oriented, manifesting events to unfold in our future, as well as based in our current behaviors.

If you research the definition of intention, it guides you to its root word, "intent." One of the definitions of intent is "the state of a person's mind that directs his or her actions toward a specific object." I found this definition to be most intriguing because it articulates a "state of…mind" that orients a person to take action toward a specific goal. But then I started thinking about the definition of "mind." I wondered if this particular definition conceptualized "mind" as only thought processes.

Intention combines thoughts and feelings. That is to say that we actually feel strong emotions, such as a passion, to create a particular intention. In addition, our rational mind helps to direct us toward actualizing this intention. Often this combination of thought and feeling can reside within us for long periods of time before we can actualize that which we desire to bring into our world. However, regardless of the time it takes, there seems to be a strong correlation with intention and actualization. People often comment on this process and say, "I always knew I would become …" or "I always knew this would occur." This "always knowing" is intention and exemplifies aligning thought and feeling in a process that culminates in realizing our intent, much like my trip to the Soviet Union was the culmination of an intention that I held for most of my life.

Intention operates on an ongoing basis as well. Each action we take has intention imbedded into the action. We are often not aware of the intention that drives the action, but it is there, motivating the action to take place. Intention precedes our behavior.

In the field of psychology, there is a concept known as "meta-message." A meta-message is the hidden or underlying meaning imbedded in a message. It may indicate something about the person delivering the message, or the true meaning of the message. The experience of a meta-message can be very uncomfortable. If the meta-message is contrary to the stated message, this can cause confusion and stress for the person receiving the message. This inconsistency, two opposing messages framed as one, can leave us feeling tentative and unsure. Often we are not aware of the meta-message. After receiving a communication, we may simply feel conflicted or unsure.

Intention can operate this way as well. We may not be aware of our own intention when we initiate a behavior or a response. Furthermore, people experiencing our behavior can be significantly influenced based on their interpretation of our intent. If they are unsure of our intention, it may well influence how they experience the event. When we do not trust an intention, we may view the behavior one way, perhaps as positive, while at the same time feeling cautious and unsure about the person or persons enacting the behavior.

For example, if a political party we generally don't support proposes a measure or a bill that appears favorable, we are very likely not to trust the intention of the act. We will consider whether there is an ulterior motive and proceed cautiously. This is an example of how our own worldview can significantly influence how we perceive a person's intention. We are most likely to distrust the intent of those about whom we hold certain opinions, prejudices, or biases.

If we operate from a place of scarcity, we will often not trust those who operate from a place of abundance. Years ago, a study was conducted to determine what segment of the population seemed most vulnerable to the influences of a cult. During the mid-seventies in Berkeley, California, various organizations (cults) would offer free meals to young people if they simply attended a gathering. The gathering would be designed to recruit the attendees into the cult. Results of the study indicated that young people who grew up in a major metropolitan city, such as New York, were less vulnerable to the influences of the cult leaders. These kids were deemed "street smart," where the motto "there's no such thing as a free lunch" applied. They were suspicious about the intent of the cult recruiters and were therefore able to withstand the influence to join the cult. This is not to suggest that operating from a place of scarcity is necessarily in our best interest. But it does demonstrate the power of our worldview.

As previously stated, every behavior must be viewed within the context in which it takes place, and intention is a powerful contextual element. When we are not aware of our intentions, we are more likely to be reactive, simply responding from automatic pilot. As we become more aware of our intentions, we can determine what is driving our thoughts, feelings, and ultimately our behavior. Being mindful of our intentions increases our awareness and can allow us to shift unwholesome intentions into more wholesome intentions.

In his book *After the Ecstasy, the Laundry*, Jack Kornfield says,

Becoming aware of intention is the key to awakening….In each situation that calls for our engagement, some inner intention will precede our response. Buddhist psychology teaches that intention is what makes the patterns of our karma. Karma, the cause and results of every action, comes from the heart's intentions that precede each action. When our intentions are kind, the karmic result is very different from when they are greedy or aggressive. If we are not aware, we will unconsciously act out of habit and fear. But if we attend to our intentions, we can notice if they spring from the body of fear or from our deliberate thoughtfulness and care.[24]

This passage suggests that our intention will actually affect our future experiences. From a Buddhist perspective, intention is the seed that will blossom into positive or negative experiences in the future.

Whether we choose to believe that intention will impact our karma, or whether we even believe in karma, it is reasonable to acknowledge that intention plays an important role in how we act in the world and how we feel about our self and the world around us. However, we must be mindful of how our intentions can create life expectations and the impact these expectations can have on us.

The Mindful Way: Intention

- Close your eyes. Begin mindful breathing. Be aware of breathing in and breathing out—just rest your awareness there.
- Now let your mind consider what your life's intentions are. Name them.
- What can you do in your life to manifest these intentions?
- Just sit with this experience.
- When you are ready, open your eyes. Write down your life's intentions and what actions may allow you to manifest them.

"What a Dump!": Life Expectations

"What a dump! What's it from, for Christ's sake....some damn Bette Davis picture, some god-damned Warner Brothers' epic?"

And with these lovely lines we meet one of the most compelling, heart-wrenching, complex, dramatic, divisive, and destructive couples ever presented in a Hollywood film. The film *Who's Afraid of Virginia Woolf?* (1966), based on the play by Edward Albee, stars Elizabeth Taylor as Martha and Richard Burton as George, and is one of Hollywood's finest screenplays.

This is a film that epitomizes dysfunctionality, power struggles, and unmet life expectations. Martha and George, having just returned home from an academic function held on the college campus where they reside, await the arrival of a young couple, Honey and Nick. Nick has just been appointed to the faculty of the college. George, a 46-year-old history professor at the college, and Martha, his 52-year-old wife and the daughter of the college president, are quite drunk.

After considerable bickering between Martha and George, and a warning from George that Martha behave in front of their guests, Martha exclaims, "I swear, if you existed, I'd divorce you." George, referencing the fact that Nick is young and good-looking, retorts, "Try to keep your clothes on, too. There aren't many more sickening sights in this world than you with a couple of drinks in you and your skirt up over your head." George continues his warning to Martha and says, "Just don't start in on the bit about the kid, that's all," a warning that defines the drama that is about to unfold.

Honey and Nick arrive and immediately feel uncomfortable, given the inebriated state of their hosts. Nonetheless they agree to stay and accept a drink. Many drinks later, George finds himself alone with Nick and asks him about the couple's plan to have children. During the conversation, Honey walks in and says, "I didn't know that you had a son...A son. I hadn't known...Tomorrow is his birthday. He will be sixteen." George asks, referring to Martha, "She told you about him?" George is obviously very upset with Martha for violating his trust by revealing to Honey a long-established secret between them.

This revelation to Honey ups the ante between George and Martha, and they engage in a destructive battle designed to destroy each other's sense of worth, a power struggle of massive proportions.

Martha humiliates and emasculates George in front of their guests, and George warns Martha that she has gone "too far" and that he will retaliate in a most convincing way. Martha says, "I stand warned...So anyway, I married the SOB. I had it all planned out. First, he'd take over the history department. Then when Daddy retired, he'd take over the whole college, you know? That was the way it was supposed to be.... Until he watched for a couple of years and started thinking that maybe it wasn't such a good idea after all, that maybe Georgie-boy didn't have the stuff, that maybe he didn't have it in him!...You see, George didn't have much push, he wasn't particularly aggressive. In fact, he was sort of a FLOP! A great big, fat FLOP! So here I am, stuck with this FLOP, this BOG in the history department."

After having endured enough of the brutality between George and Martha, Nick asserts that it's time for him and his wife to leave. In the wee hours of the morning and in a drunken stupor, George, with Martha seated in the passenger seat, begins to drive them home. On their way, Honey spots a sign that reads "Red Basket Cocktails—Dancing" and insists that they stop and go dancing.

As Martha dances seductively with Nick, she continues her humiliation of George and says, "Well, Georgie-boy had lots of big ambitions. In spite of something funny in his past...Which Georgie-boy here turned into a novel...His first attempt and also his last...But Daddy took a look at Georgie's novel...And he was very shocked by what he read...A novel all about a naughty boy-child...Who...killed his mother and his father dead. And Daddy said, 'Look here, I will not let you publish such a thing...'"

George jumps up and yells, "Stop it, Martha; the game is over."

But Martha continues and says, "Just imagine, a book all about a boy who murders his mother and kills his father and pretends it's all an accident...And do you want to know the clincher? Do you want to know what big, brave Georgie said to Daddy?...Georgie said... 'But Daddy, I mean...but Sir, this isn't a novel at all...this is the truth...this really happened...To me!'"

George assaults Martha, strangling her as he calls her a "satanic bitch." Nick grabs George and throws him to the floor, as the innkeeper tells them to leave.

They return to the house. As the sun begins to rise, in front of their guests, George says to Martha, "Sweetheart, I'm afraid I've got some bad news for you—for both of us, I mean. Some rather sad news...I'm afraid our boy isn't coming home for his birthday... Our son is dead. He was killed late in the afternoon on a country road with his learner's permit in his pocket, as he swerved to avoid a porcupine, and drove straight into a large tree...I thought you should know."

"You cannot do that," Martha responds. "You can't decide these things for yourself! I will not let you do that. I will not let you decide these things. No. You can't kill him. You can't let him die."

Nick, witnessing this final encounter, finally realizes that George and Martha never had a son, and that they had invented this story of an imaginary son to cope with the devastating disappointment of not being able to have a child.

Unmet Life Expectations

For twenty years, I have shown this film to my psychology students. As an assignment, I have asked them to analyze the film and diagnose Martha and George, develop a treatment plan for this couple, and identify the essential problem, or "the bottom line," between this couple. For twenty years, students have successfully identified the issues of alcohol, have defended their diagnoses of Martha and George, and have even developed some reasonable treatment plans designed to treat this couple. However, what their responses consistently lack is an assessment of the magnitude of this couple's inability to meet each other's life expectations and the emotional devastation this has caused.

Martha and George had a contract: partly overt, partly covert. They were not only to make each other happy, they were to bolster each other's sense of being, their sense of worth. Martha's inner world and her self-esteem crumbled as a result of not being able to bear a child. George's inner world was affected by this as well, but what truly affected his self-esteem was when "Daddy" forbade him to publish his novel at the cost of his job. George "caved in," never attempted to publish his novel, and lost a great deal of confidence and self-worth.

Life's disappointments were so great for Martha and George that these disappointments not only led to their alcoholic ways, but led to intense anger and even hatred towards one another. Martha and George develop an imaginary son designed to maintain a system of denial and somehow contain the enormity of their pain. But, as is the case with most illusions, eventually the illusion broke down and the pain overwhelmed.

And this doesn't only happen in the movies.

Life Expectations and Depression

*Woe to him, when the day of his dreams finally came, found it to be
so different from all that he had longed for!*
                                   Viktor Frankl, *Man's Search for Meaning*[25]

I have treated many people who have suffered from depression. These days most therapists seem to be oriented to using some kind of medication to help this situation, and why not? There has been marked improvement in the medications that are available to help depression. Medication intervention is based on an understanding that there is a change in the chemical makeup in the brain, specifically in what are known as neurotransmitters. Neurotransmitters relay signals between neurons and cells. They "ferry" information (electrical impulses) between neurons. Changes in neurotransmitters can affect mood. Medication intervention is designed to correct or modify these chemical changes and alleviate depression. What causes these chemical changes in the brain is a subject of debate.

Psychological theorists have presented various explanations regarding the cause of depression. Given the variety of explanations, there appears to be no clear understanding or consensus regarding what ultimately causes depression. One factor that I have consistently observed in my depressed clients is a sense of significant disappointment in life as a result of unfulfilled life expectations. This disappointment seems to lead to a fundamental experience that life is meaningless.

Consider the following story. A well-groomed, well-dressed, forty-six-year-old man came to my office. After some formalities that needed to be covered, I asked him, "So, what brings you here today?" He responded by telling me the following story.

"Last night, when I got home from a professional conference I was attending, I went straight into my study. It was late. My wife and kids were asleep. I poured myself a drink of brandy and sat and stared blankly for what seemed an eternity. Eventually, I got up, walked over to my desk, and opened the drawer where I keep my gun. I took it out and laid it on the table in front of me. I sat down at my desk, took out the ammo box, and put it next to the gun. I took out a single bullet and ran it through my fingers for a while. I loaded the gun, picked it up, and held it, all the while thinking, 'Go ahead, just do it. Put the gun to your head and do it. Everybody will be better off. What are you, a chicken shit? Do it already and it will all be over with.' Just then I heard my baby cry. My wife got up to go to the baby's room. I put the gun away and called you first thing in the morning."

Whatever got him to this desperate place? Here was a man who appeared to have it all. He was living the American dream. He was a successful physician, the chief of staff at a prominent hospital, and made lots of money. He was married to a beautiful woman, had two children, lived in a beautiful house in an affluent community, and drove a BMW. However, he hated his life, hated himself, and hated how he behaved towards his family, particularly towards his wife. He was despondent.

We worked together for some time. It wasn't easy, and there were several scary moments. But eventually, as we pieced together what this had been about for him, he started to shift his priorities and change his life in a positive direction.

This is an all-too-familiar story: perhaps not to this magnitude, but more common than one might think. Let's examine why a successful, well-educated, professional family man could feel so lost. Look at the words I have chosen to use to describe him: "successful," "well-educated," "professional," "family man." All of these words have a common theme in our culture. They are all descriptors of life achievements that are supposed to lead to happiness. Success is a good thing. Education is a good thing. Being a professional and being a family man are good things. So why would they lead to despondency and depression?

If you look at my client's life journey, you will uncover a pattern that is highly supported by our culture. This pattern can be illustrated by the cliché "eye on the prize." We are aware that people who are oriented towards instant gratification, or the need to be satisfied now, and forego any thought of the future or future consequences can experience significant difficulties in their life due to impulsive behavior. So we teach our children to delay their gratification. We say things like, "You can't eat dessert until you finish your dinner," "A penny saved is a penny earned," and a host of other sayings designed to help our children to learn to delay their gratification.

Delaying gratification is a necessary component of long-term success and usually happiness. But what happens when we delay, and delay, and delay, and when we finally obtain "the prize," the prize is not what we expected it to be? What happens when we forgo the joy of the journey, focused only on reaching the goal, and the goal is unsatisfying? One thing that can happen is depression, particularly if the effort and time put into obtaining the goal is significant.

My client had spent his whole life with one thing in mind: to become a doctor. And this choice was not his alone, if it was his at all. His parents loved the idea of "my son, the doctor" and, on both a conscious level and a covert level, pushed him towards the goal. He was led to believe that life would be good if he simply could accomplish this goal. He willingly pursued the goal. But once he reached it, he was desperately disappointed. He found himself feeling overwhelmingly burdened by responsibility. Nothing in his life felt joyous. And the more he felt this way, the more miserable he became, and the more miserable he made everyone around him feel. That night, after a particularly boring, self-aggrandizing conference, he reached his boiling point. "No more," he said to himself, but unfortunately how he was choosing to enact "no more" was self-destructive.

The film *Born on the Fourth of July*, starring Tom Cruise, illustrates how life's expectations can lead us astray and leave us feeling enraged and disappointed. The film is based on the true story of a bright, attractive, popular young man, the type of young man who is on the high school wrestling team, gets all the pretty girls, and has a very bright future. Fiercely patriotic, the pride of his family, he foregoes college to join the military to fight in Vietnam. Based on his expectations, he is beside himself with excitement. He can't wait to get to Vietnam and "see some action." Unfortunately for him, he does. He gets shot and is paralyzed from the waist down. But that is not what this film or his story is all about. This is a story about transformation. This is a story about how easily influenced we are by our family, or our country, or the media, all telling us who to be and how to live. "Love it or leave it." That's what the posters said. If you don't agree with the political view of the government, then get out. What happened to "question authority" as a means of encouraging critical thinking and supporting autonomy?

What we see in this film is the maturation and transformation of this young man. Upon his return from Vietnam, wheelchair bound, and after tremendous personal reflection, he becomes one of the leading opponents of the war. He travels from high school to high school, urging other young men and women not to fall prey to the propaganda about the glory of war. He becomes such a staunch opponent of the war that he is vilified by the supporters of the war.

These examples are not presented here to advocate an anti-war stance, or to underscore the burdens and responsibilities that often come with success and status. These examples are presented to demonstrate the emotional impact our delusional thinking can have on us. And by delusional I mean "a false belief," a belief that when we get x, or when we attain y, we will be happy. This belief system is based on external validation and attachment. It is the belief that there is something out there that will make us happy, rather than the recognition that there is something already within us that will bring meaning and contentment to our existence.

It should not be simply the view from the top of the mountain that motivates us to take the climb. If that were the case, we would simply take transport to the top, see the view, and depart (and sometimes we do). There is something in the climb that motivates us to do the climb.

There is something in the challenge that allows us to continue the climb. Metaphorically, the mountain is the sundae and the view is the cherry on top. The mountain resides in all of us.

The Mindful Way: Expectations

- Close your eyes. Begin mindful breathing. Be aware of breathing in and breathing out—just rest your awareness there.
- Now bring your awareness to any unmet expectations you have in your life.
- Name them by:
  - *Recognizing* what they are.
  - *Accepting* the truth of how things are.
  - *Investigating* what they are about for you.
  - *Non-identifying* with the outcome of these expectations.
- Just sit with this experience and allow yourself to experience the unhappiness these unmet expectations have caused.
- Now ask yourself, "Do I have to hold onto these expectations?"
- Breathing in and breathing out, open your heart and feel compassion for yourself.
- Now say aloud, "Let them go." Say this for as long as you need.
- Now bring your awareness to a life unbound by these expectations.
- Sit with this experience.
- When you are ready, open your eyes.

Chapter Nine

Honoring the Master: Anxiety

Many years ago, in a far-off destination, deep in the mountains of India, a celebration was held. A noble master was to be honored for his life's dedication to teaching spiritual enlightenment. His monastery was filled with excitement as his disciples went about preparing for the festive day. This day was to be a very special occasion, because the master was to be honored by one of the great masters of his time.

A great feast was prepared, and all gathered as the festivities were about to begin. The master was given the seat of honor as his distinguished guest began the ceremonies. Great praise was given to the master, and all that were present acknowledged their love and devotion to him. The day was a great success. Everyone's hard work had been rewarded by "a perfect day."

In the wee hours of the morning, the master's number-one disciple heard rumblings emanating from outside of his window. He quickly rose from his slumber and peered out into the awakening dawn. There he saw his master walking into the forest, rucksack on his back.

The disciple quickly ran after his master and, upon catching up to him, exclaimed, "Master, where are you going?" The master replied, "Into the wood to sit in silence."

"But why, Master?" asked the disciple.

"Because today I have failed," answered the master.

"Failed?" asked the disciple. "But what do you mean? Today was a wonderful success. Everything went as planned and our honored guest bestowed the most wonderful blessings upon you."

"Yes, number-one disciple, all that you say is true."

"So, what, then?" asked the disciple.

The master looked at his disciple with great concentration and, after a few moments of reflection, said, "As our honored guest was bestowing blessings upon me and our lovely home, I looked down upon my hands and realized that my palms were sweating. I have much work to do."

Anxiety

"My palms were sweating." After a lifetime of meditation and devotional practice, our enlightened master had sweaty palms. Even the wise old sage is not immune to anxiety. But this is not the essential moral of this story. The true moral of the story is the master's desire to return to a place of calm and nonattachment. The path he chose was to concentrate on his "inner life" through silence and meditation.

Anxiety lives in all of us. It stimulates our sympathetic nervous system, which is responsible for our "fight or flight" response. It serves us by indicating that we are perceiving a threat in our environment, and we should take appropriate precautions to deal with it. It can heighten our alertness, allowing us to respond quickly to an adverse situation. It can serve as a motivator, in that a little anxiety may heighten our attention to detail and improve our performance. And it can be a source for change. For example, when we experience a "nagging feeling" that something is not right or not satisfying, it can motivate us to take action to alleviate these feelings.

However, it's a very slippery slope. While too little anxiety may cause us not to notice that there is potential danger in our midst and prevent us from responding appropriately, a significant amount of anxiety can negatively affect our performance. In fact, too much anxiety can immobilize us all together: the "deer in the headlight" response. Millions of Americans are medicated to ward off the negative effects of anxiety and maintain a reasonable level of functionality.

Anxiety affects who we are and how we behave in the world. It manifests in ways that are not always obvious. We tend to focus on the obvious manifestations of anxiety: a funny feeling in our stomach, quickened heart rate, increased sweating, worry, etc. What is not obvious is the impact that our ever-present "underlying anxiety" has on us.

Underlying anxiety is part of our emotional context and originates from our resistance to accept impermanence. We all construct ways to contain our anxiety, both on a conscious level (leaving to go to the airport several hours early so we will not miss our plane) and on an unconscious level (our defense mechanisms, or psychological strategies to cope with reality). However, when these fail, anxiety bubbles up to the surface, and we have the emotional experience we know to be anxiety.

Most often we concentrate on the external causes of anxiety and don't pay much attention to the underlying anxiety we carry around with us on a daily basis. We may be quick to determine what is causing us to be anxious, and we will often take measures to eliminate the external factor or factors creating the anxiety. We believe that the external stimulus is causing the anxiety, and, once it's removed, we will no longer be anxious.

For example, if we are walking along a path and encounter a snake in the middle of the road, we may experience anxiety, particularly if we are afraid of snakes. Once the snake is removed or simply slithers away, our anxiety is likely to diminish. This is all well and good. However, our attachment to this cause-and-effect scenario (I see a snake—it makes me anxious—the snake is removed—I am no longer anxious) is also deceptive.

The deception lies in our attachment to the belief that it is *only* the external circumstance that is causing the anxiety. As a means of survival our brain is actually constructed to constantly scan our environment for signs of danger and lets us know through the experience of anxiety that danger exists. This orients us towards our "outer life." We believe that if we simply eliminate the external source of anxiety, either through removing an object (the snake) or through obtaining an object (i.e., money), we will eliminate anxiety. As a result of this process we tend to overlook the impact that our underlying anxiety is having on our experience, and we focus on our outer life rather than our inner life.

Each of us carries with us some level of anxiety. Anxiety is like an emotional reservoir. How full the reservoir is will influence how easily our anxiety surfaces. If, for example, we measure anxiety on a scale of one to ten, one being very low anxiety and ten being very high anxiety, a person functioning at level nine will easily become anxious (remember the client I described in chapter 5, who became extremely anxious because her boss did not say "good morning"?). However, if a person is functioning at level two, it will take a more significant stimulus to manifest anxiety.

Imagine a rain barrel filled to the brim. It will take very little rain for the barrel to begin to overflow. Now imagine a rain barrel that is practically empty. It would take a raging storm before the barrel filled and overflowed. Metaphorically speaking, each of us have our own internal rain barrel, but instead of being filled with water, it is filled with anxiety. For some of us, the barrel remains fairly empty; for others, it is filled to the brim. This is why we can each react so differently to the exact same anxiety-producing external event. The external event pulls from us the anxiety that resides within. It is more difficult to make a Buddha-like person anxious, because they have let go of many of the elements that cause us to feel anxious. Conversely, it is very easy to make a highly anxious person more anxious, because they are filled to the brim with anxiety.

The relevance of understanding this is profound. Why? Because so many of us are focused on alleviating the external factors that cause us to be anxious. We attempt to make more money or get a better job, a better house, a better car, or a better spouse, all in the service of making us feel more secure and less anxious. However, even after we have acquired all that we believed we needed to feel secure, we still feel anxious. And if we are unsuccessful at acquiring all those things, we simply continue to believe that if we could acquire them, we would feel better. Either way, it's a trap. We can't eliminate our anxiety from the outside; we must tackle our anxiety from within. We must focus our attention on our inner life while appropriately attending to external demands. This is why practicing meditation, yoga, t'ai chi, or any other activity that concentrates on our inner life, and helps discipline the mind and calm the body, is so helpful. The body cannot be physiologically anxious and non-anxious at the same time. Calm the mind, relax the body, and anxiety will begin to dissipate.

The Mind and Anxiety

As we have discussed, often it is an external event that produces an experience of anxiety. But it could just as easily be brought up by a thought that is not attached to an external event. In fact, when we experience anxiety (or, for that matter, when we experience anything), we are always reacting to the environment of our mind. Our mind creates our experience. Sometimes the mind interprets reality based on what it believes it has observed from the outside environment (perception), and other times it is simply responding to a current thought pattern that is completely independent from the outside environment. When our thoughts overwhelm us by imagining the worst, or by continuously bombarding us, or by focusing on a constant source of worry, we will often be filled with anxiety. The interesting thing about this process is that our thoughts, and even our perceptions, might not be based in reality at all. But that really doesn't matter. All that matters is that we perceive it or think it, and we react to it.

The mind thinks what it thinks, and perceives what it perceives regardless of the authenticity of the thing being observed or thought about. Consider a mirage. The mind perceives a desert oasis when there is none. Or try to convince someone living in 500 AD that the world wasn't flat, or the earth wasn't the center of the universe.

The mind is a powerful observer. We even dismiss our sensory experience if it doesn't fit with what the mind expects. For example, studies have shown that when subjects were given a taste of vanilla yogurt mixed with flavorless red food coloring and packaged as "strawberry yogurt," the overwhelming majority of the subjects identified the taste as strawberry, not vanilla.

When the mind is troubled, when the mind is filled with negative thoughts, the body responds with anxiety. The body is where anxiety resides. Calm the mind, and the body will follow. Upset the mind, and the body will carry anxiety. For example, high amounts of stress and anxiety result in the body's production of abnormal amounts of cortisol, a hormone produced by the adrenal gland, often referred to as the "stress hormone." High levels of cortisol have been associated with many negative side effects, including high blood pressure, cognitive impairment, blood sugar imbalances, lower immunity, and abdominal fat, which is associated with heart disease and strokes.

How does this underlying anxiety develop? To understand this, perhaps we should start at the beginning: that is to say, the beginning of one's life experience.

In the Beginning

How does a baby experience the world? Given the power of our *thinking* mind, it is difficult to imagine how we experienced the world in a precognitive state (a state without thought) residing only in our *non-thinking* mind. How did we make sense of the world without the internal dialogue of words and categories? How can we even imagine this state of being, if even our imagining uses words and concepts to imagine this state? Fortunately, words can describe a state of being, even if during that state of being there was no cognitive functioning or language to define our world.

Simply put, the baby *feels* his or her way through life. The baby has a continuous sensation of life's experience registered through the body as feelings. This sensation can be summarized into two basic categories of experience: calm (non-anxious) or distressed (anxious). That's it. Either the baby is feeling calm or distressed. Early Buddhist writings suggest three states of being: unpleasant, neutral, or pleasant. If the state of "neutral" is by definition a non-anxious state, then we are still left with only two states of being: calm or distressed. This is our original experience, our original ground of being.

Calm versus Distressed

We have all begun this journey of life as simply feeling beings, not thinking beings. Cognitive functioning (language, categorization, constructs, etc.) develops as our brain develops and matures. Our thinking mind develops in part as a response to our extreme vulnerability and helplessness as an infant. It is part of our survival instinct, categorizing the world so we can understand our environment and develop coping strategies to maximize our survival. Eventually our thinking mind becomes the dominant mechanism through which we experience the world. Even though we may all know some people who have never mastered the art of thinking, as evidenced by their behavior and thought processes, many more of us tend to over-rely on cognitive functioning to process the world while we under-utilize our natural, original processing mechanism of feeling. Feeling informs our intuitive process, and without the appropriate balance between rationality and intuition, we cannot maximize our world experience. It is as if we travel through the world with one hand tied behind our back.

Let's get back to our baby, who is processing the world through feeling. Either the baby is calm or distressed. A distressed baby is an anxious baby. It doesn't matter how distressed; what matters is that the baby is not in a place of calm. A distressed baby cries, or fidgets, or expresses discomfort in some way to rally the environment to help it return to a place of comfort. All the baby experiences is a sense of discomfort. And all the baby wants is to return to a place of calm (as did the master with sweaty palms). But, unlike the master, the baby is helpless to do this on its own. The baby does not possess the internal fortitude to comfort itself. The baby needs the outside world to intervene to change its experience. The baby needs "mother," or whomever may be available, to bring comfort and calm to its experience.

So, what does mother or caretaker do to try to restore order and calm to the baby? She likely does several things. She might begin by simply providing a sense of comfort to the baby. She might hold the baby, enveloping the baby with warmth. She might rock the baby, sing to the baby, feed the baby, or gently pat the baby in a soothing manner. If these approaches are unsuccessful, she is likely to search for an irritant that has caused the baby to react in this manner. She might check the baby's diaper to see if the baby needs changing. She might check the environment to determine if it's too cold or too hot, or too noisy or chaotic. She might try to determine if the baby is ill.

If she is able to identify a likely cause for the baby's discomfort, she will make an effort to resolve the cause to return the baby back to a state of calm. If this approach is still unsuccessful, she is likely to try distraction. She may hold up and shake a rattle, or make a funny face, or turn on a musical toy. Anything that might distract the baby's attention long enough so the baby refocuses and is no longer distressed. This method can be effective, as long as a substantial irritant doesn't persist.

For many of us, this cycle doesn't change. Although we mature and develop, often our response to distress is similar to how we reacted as a baby. When we feel distressed, we often seek comfort from others. Often times we try to identify the irritant and "fix" the problem (men love to do this). Other times, and all too often in modern-day culture, we use distraction. We use alcohol, drugs, sex, adrenaline, TV, our job, or any source of distraction that may work. The problem is that these methods simply mask the stress and anxiety, and the distraction itself can become problematic (i.e., addictions). They ultimately don't reduce the distress; they substantiate its existence.

Imagine that you have a young child who, in the middle of the night, calls out from his bed, terrified that there is a ghost in his closet. You run to comfort him, but he is not easily comforted. So, what to do? How would you ultimately deal with this situation? Here are the facts: the boy is afraid because there is a ghost in his closet. Given that the closet is the problem (because there is a ghost in there), why not padlock the closet doors? What a great solution! You can go out and buy the heftiest padlock, chain the doors together, padlock the chain, and throw away the key. Voilà, problem solved. Or is it? It is true that the boy might feel safer knowing, and seeing, that the closet is padlocked. But what have we actually accomplished by padlocking the closet? The answer may be obvious. We have assured this young boy that a ghost really does exist in this closet, and he has every right to be afraid. This is how we substantiate a fear, instead of reducing and ridding ourselves of a fear. And that same principle exists when we use distraction as a method to deal with our anxiety. It may give us some sense of relief or comfort, but in the end all it does is substantiate our anxiety.

Understanding the baby's journey is crucial to understanding our own overall journey through life. Unlike certain animals who are born fully functional and independent (like the baby sea turtle), the human baby animal is completely dependent on its environment for its survival. Leave a newborn baby unattended, and it will not survive. Attend only to a baby's physical needs, and its psychological development will be impaired, as demonstrated by the following studies.

Harlow's Monkeys and the Preemies

In what has become one of the most famous psychological studies, Harry Harlow conducted an experiment using Rhesus monkeys to determine the influence that touch, warmth, and contact would have on the emergence of psychological well-being. Essentially, Harlow removed baby monkeys from their mothers and placed them in two similar environments with one crucial difference. One group of monkeys was provided a surrogate mother figure made of wire, while the other group was offered a surrogate mother figure made of wire ensconced in terry cloth. Each group was provided appropriate nutrition. Harlow observed that the group of monkeys that had been given a terry-cloth mother figure clung to this figure on an ongoing basis, regardless of whether the figure was providing food through a baby bottle containing milk. The other group of monkeys, provided with a wire mother figure only, made contact only during feeding, because that was where the milk bottle had been placed.

Various scenarios were created to observe the reactions of both groups of monkeys. For example, each group was placed in an unfamiliar room. The monkeys who lived with a terry-cloth mother figure froze in fear, or cried and screamed to be reunited with their mother figure. The other group of monkeys reacted with blank stares and a general demeanor of "disassociation."

In another scenario, a frightening object was introduced into the monkey's "home" environment. The terry-cloth monkeys clung tightly to their mother figure, searching for comfort and security. The other group of monkeys cowered in the corner of the room.

The overall conclusion of this study was that contact and connection with a primary love object is essential to the psychological well-being of a primate, and that the absence of such a connection will severely impair psychological development and contribute to increased anxiety, resulting in pathological functioning.

Decades later, a study was conducted with premature babies. Once again, two groups were formed. Each group was given the exact level of care to ensure survival and wellness. The environment (the incubators in which these babies lived), the feeding schedule, and the overall quality of care was exactly the same. However, one group of babies received one additional factor: the factor of touch. In this group each baby received a specific number of hand "strokes" delivered on a precise schedule until the baby was released from the hospital. Two years later, both groups were evaluated. Findings revealed that the group that received no stroking was smaller in both height and weight, had a smaller brain circumference, and developmentally generally lagged behind the other group. Hail, the power of touch.

Psychological Development

So what are the significant characteristics of the infant's journey? Other than wanting to help an infant navigate this journey, why should we as adults, who have already passed through this journey, really care? How will understanding this journey help us now? We have all been through it and seem to have survived. Or have we?

After many years of teaching graduate students in clinical psychology, it seems clear to me that most of us never gain appropriate insight about our psychological development. It's not taught in primary school. It's not usually discussed at home. We seem to understand that self-esteem is an important variable in the overall development of psychological health, but many of us don't really know what it is, let alone how we get it. In fact, Harlow's monkey experiments came about, in part, as a result of the belief that too much contact was overindulgent and not good for psychological development. (That viewpoint must have been developed by a psychologist who had a smothering mother.) Harlow described these experiments as a study of "love" and actually revealed his findings to the American Psychological Association in an address entitled "The Nature of Love." There is no such thing as too much love. It is what we all seek, and, even more, it is what we all crave to give.

To understand our psychological development, the development of self-esteem, and the relationship between self-esteem and anxiety (the way we deal with stress), we need to go back to the infant's journey.

Consider the fact that life begins as a tiny particle, an embryo, within the human body. There is no differentiation between that particle and the body in which it is housed. The embryo matures and develops into a fetus, and still remains part of the body. The birth process is the initial step that separates the baby from its mother. Why do I say "initial step"? Because, although the baby is separated physically from the mother's body, psychologically and emotionally, the baby is still attached to the mother. This has been referred to as "occupying the same orbit" as the mother, and it suggests that the baby has no awareness of being a separate human being.

However, the baby is a separate human being, with the same needs that it had prior to the birth experience. It needs sustenance, warmth, and a sense of security, which the enveloping womb provided. But no longer will the baby's needs be automatically taken care of, as they were in the womb. Now there will be a delay in need gratification. Now the baby will have to signal the mother to create an awareness in the mother that its needs need attending to. And what is the crucial element of this process, the process that motivates the baby to "call out" to the mother? Discomfort. When the baby shifts emotionally from a calm place to a distressed place, it will let the universe know.

Attunement

A fundamental element of the dance between infant and mother is the degree to which the mother is attuned to her infant. Attunement is an intuitive process, some would say an unconscious process, in which mother and child are aligned (attuned) to each other's energy. An example of attunement can be demonstrated by a process that often takes place with breastfeeding mothers, the manner in which the mother's breasts fill with milk. What is interesting about this process is that some of the time the baby's cry of hunger causes the mother's breasts to fill with milk, at other times the mother's breasts filling with milk cause the baby to cry with hunger, and yet at other times both occur at the same time. In any case, there clearly seems to be an energetic connection between mother and baby that informs both mother and baby. In essence, they "feel" each other.

It has been theorized that attunement can influence the well-being of the infant, both from a physiological and psychological basis. It is obvious how this process can affect the physiological aspects of the infant. The baby will suffer if the mother does not tune into the physiological needs of the infant and provide food, shelter, and warmth.

But how does this process affect the baby's psychological development and functioning? This may be less obvious. Let us remember the basic tenor of attunement, that of mother and infant connecting on an energetic level. As discussed earlier, the infant simply experiences the world from a feeling level. It has yet to develop cognition to think about its environment. The infant feels the environment. The infant not only feels environmental factors such as hot and cold, or loud and quiet, but experiences the environment as being either calm (safe) or stressful (fearful).

A major part of the infant's environment is the mother. If the mother is anxious or stressed, the baby may pick up this emotion and can experience this anxiety. Remember, mother and infant inhabit a single orbit. The baby is not aware of being a separate being. The mother has plenty to feel anxious about. It is an awesome responsibility to care for a newborn, particularly if it is the mother's first child.

Most babies, at first, are unable to self-soothe. That is to say that the baby does not have the emotional constitution to calm itself, to move itself from a distressed place to a calm place. This will come with time, and there is tremendous individual variability regarding when this develops. For example, determinants such as temperament and personality, even at this age, play a significant role in how the infant relates to the environment.

Some babies are what are known as "low-threshold" babies, while others are categorized as "high-threshold" babies. Low-threshold babies require less stimulation from the environment to react. They tend to be alert, somewhat restless, and often more difficult because they are more reactive. They are very responsive and require little stimulation to become responsive. High-threshold babies are just the opposite. They require more stimulation before they respond. They tend to be the "easy baby." Environmental stimuli don't easily affect them, so they can tolerate much more prior to reacting. These physiological "attitudes" seem to be innate and part of the overall temperament of an infant from birth. As a result of being more reactive to their environment, low-threshold babies may require more comforting. They are more likely to react more frequently, and often their reaction will be from an anxious place. But whether high threshold or low threshold, whenever her baby is distressed, the mother's response is to bring a sense of comfort, a sense of security, to her baby.

Caregivers who are more fully attuned to their babies are able to navigate the process of responding to their babies more effectively. They tend to intuitively know the level of need their baby has at any given moment. They modify their reaction to their baby accordingly. As a result, they support the process needed for the baby to learn how to self-soothe, which is the *seed* of self-esteem, which is discussed in the next chapter. Infants who are able to self-soothe actually feel more secure, because they can rely on themselves and be less dependent on their environment. This is an empowering experience and begins the development of autonomy (self-reliance), which is a contributing factor in the development of self-esteem. They will spend more time feeling calm and be more able to return to a state of calm when distressed. But how exactly does this self-soothing mechanism develop?

Self-Soothing

Let us first take a simplistic view of this process. If you own a dog and you want to teach the dog to sit on command, you are likely to take a behavioral approach. A behavioral approach is based on a reinforcement model. Positive behavior (the behavior you want) is reinforced and rewarded. So you might stand in front of your dog and verbalize the command, "Sit." At first you might have to actually assist the dog to sit by applying gentle downward pressure to its hindquarters while saying the word "sit." Each time the dog sits, you reward the dog by giving the dog a small treat. You repeat this process over and over, rewarding the dog with a treat each time the dog sits on command. Eventually, with time, patience, and determination, the dog sits on command.

What we know as psychologists is that the fastest way to create a learned behavior is by rewarding that behavior every time it occurs (positive reinforcement). Parents should remember this, because punishment is a very poor way to create a positive behavior. Each time the dog sits (or in the beginning, each time the dog motions towards sitting), we give the dog a treat. This method of reinforcing behavior after every positive behavior is known as "continuous reinforcement." However, once the behavior is learned, continuous reinforcement is not the best method to ensure that the behavior will continue indefinitely. The best method to ensure that the behavior will continue indefinitely is called "intermittent reinforcement." During intermittent reinforcement, we do not reward the behavior each time it occurs. We reward the behavior some of the time. And the trick is estimating how long a behavior will continue before you have to reward it to avoid the "extinguishing" of the behavior. In other words, how far can we go without rewarding a particular behavior before the behavior just stops?

Imagine that the dog's ability to sit on command is newly established. The dog has been trained by being rewarded by a treat after every time he has sat on command. Now you choose to change the rules. You command the dog to sit, and he does. However, this time you don't give the dog a treat. The dog rises. Once again, you command him to sit and he does. Once again, you do not reward him. How many times can you repeat this process before the dog simply stops sitting on command? The ideal situation (which we rarely know) is to reward the behavior just before it's about to extinguish. For example, if by the sixth command the dog has not been rewarded, the dog may feel quite frustrated with these developments. The dog may opt to try this behavior one more time. If not rewarded after this next sit, he will quit participating in this behavior. On the seventh command to sit, the dog sits, and this time you give the dog a treat. You have just bought yourself a whole new series of positive behavior. Perhaps next time, the dog can last up to twelve behaviors before it needs to be reinforced. Eventually, you may have to rarely reinforce the behavior, and you can even change the reinforcer. You might change the reinforcer from a treat to praise. It is certainly helpful to pair the new reinforcer (praise) with the original reinforcer (a treat). If each time you give the dog a treat you praise him as well, your ability to substitute praise as a reinforcer instead of a treat will increase.

Aren't we all subject to this kind of influence? The entire gaming industry is based on this model of shaping behavior. Have you ever been to Las Vegas and played a slot machine? If so, you've probably noticed that when someone in a casino wins a sizable jackpot at a slot machine, the machine sets off all kinds of bells and whistles. These bells and whistles are a reinforcer. They are timed to go off intermittently to ensure that you keep gambling. It doesn't matter if you have won. What matters is that someone has won and you have been made aware of that fact. Subconsciously, you are now drawn back to the machines to try to win a jackpot.

Let's get back to our mother-baby dynamic. Essentially the process I described above is the process that goes on between mother and baby. Each time the baby is distressed, the baby lets the mother know, either overtly (crying) or covertly (the mother just has a "feeling" based on a shift in baby's energy). The mother responds by providing comfort to the baby, which in turn allows the baby to move from being distressed to being calm. The baby's anxiety, or discomfort, prompts the mother to respond with an attempt to comfort the baby. Sometimes the attempt is successful, sometimes not. However, with consistency, the mother's response to the baby to provide comfort acts as a positive reinforcer. The baby responds by calming down and moving into a calm state. With repeated exposure to this dance, mother and baby develop a mechanism to restore calm when needed. Over time, this continuous reinforcer, the mother responding each time the baby is distressed, changes to an intermittent reinforcer. The mother may choose to delay her response, may be unable to respond, or simply choose not to respond at all to see if the baby can self-soothe. As with our dog learning to sit on command, too little reinforcement (the mother not responding to her baby's needs on a continuous basis) will not create the desired effect, and too much reinforcement (the mother not allowing baby a chance to self-soothe) will create an atmosphere that can lead to rapid extinction of the behavior.

Think about a baby "learning" to sleep through the night. In the beginning, primarily due to the baby's need to eat, the baby cannot sleep through the night. In fact, most babies will wake several times during the night. The mother (or caretaker) responds to the baby's need. Over time, as the baby develops, matures, and increases in size, the baby's ability to go longer without having to be fed increases. Many babies, some as early as three or four months old, have the capacity to go at least six hours, and often more, without the need to be fed. However, a pattern of interaction has been established, one that usually has multiple visits to the baby during the night. Just because the baby's need to feed in the middle of the night no longer exists doesn't mean that the baby's need for contact has changed. Often the baby will still cry out, and how the baby is responded to at this point can often be a point of contention between couples and theorists alike. Some say "let the baby cry," intimating that the baby will eventually go back to sleep (usually the father). Others contend that if the baby is crying, the baby needs the assistance and comfort of the caregiver (usually Mom).

Most parents take a middle-of-the-road approach, an approach that, based on our reinforcement model, is probably the most effective approach. The middle-of-the-road approach is to delay the response. That is to say, while the baby is crying, the caregiver waits to respond, and if the baby does not stop crying at a certain point, then he or she attends to the baby. This process may continue for quite a while, sometimes several weeks or even months. Gradually the delay between the caregiver's response and the baby's initial crying becomes longer and longer. This response is an important milestone in the development of the infant. The baby is "forced" to deal with its discomfort for a longer period of time, by itself, even though eventually comfort is provided by the caregiver. This serves to reassure the baby that comfort is forthcoming. The interesting part of this new dance between caregiver and the baby is eventually the "forthcoming comfort" is provided by the baby.

Over time, the baby actually becomes more self-reliant. Let me repeat this: the baby becomes more self-reliant. That's it. That is what it's all about. That is our task as parents, to build and nurture self-reliance. The more an individual is emotionally self-reliant, the more calm and less anxious the individual.

A parent that smothers a child and does not encourage the child to rely on his or her self will support anxiety. A parent who is inattentive and does not provide the necessary love, attention, and connectedness needed by a child to feel secure will also support anxiety. As stated earlier, all children are not alike and should not be related to as if they are. Knowing your child and responding to the specific needs of that child is paramount to a successful child-rearing journey.

Internal Attunement

Dr. Dan Siegel, a leading authority on mindfulness and the brain, discusses the role of attunement in his book *The Mindful Brain*. He talks about the benefits of being "internally attuned" and a concept known as "interoception," which he describes as "a process in which we perceive inward—using what we've called our 'sixth sense' so we can come to sense what we are feeling in our body." He asserts that each of us needs to be attuned to our own inner self to be available to be attuned to others.[26]

To illustrate this process, I would like to share an experience I had while attending a dog show.

The dog show was held at a very large venue configured in the following way. In the center of the venue was an arena surrounded by seats. This is where the owners proudly displayed their dogs. Surrounding the arena were several large warehouse-type halls in which the dogs were housed by breed. The general public had complete access to these halls, and in fact, the fun part of this experience was the ability to move from hall to hall and interact with the dogs, which is exactly what I did.

Towards the end of the day, I finally made my way to the last of these halls. As I walked through the tunnel that led to the entrance of the hall, I was struck by "a feeling." The energy seemed different. I couldn't see or hear anything. Something just felt different, and not in a calm and loving way. I continued my approach, entered through the main doors, and there I stood at the gateway to a room filled with the large (aggressive) breed dogs. I love dogs. But faced with a room filled with Dobermans, German Shepherds, Malamutes, etc., I could feel a difference. I felt that difference before entering the room and before any noticeable environmental cues could inform me of the environment. I was attuned to my environment, and my "sixth sense" allowed my intuitive process to do its job.

When a mother is attuned to herself, she is better able to be attuned to her baby's needs and provide the comfort and security necessary for healthy psychological development. When we are attuned to ourselves, we are better able to attune to others, which is the seed of compassion.

The Mindful Way: Attunement

- Close your eyes. Begin mindful breathing. Be aware of breathing in and breathing out—just rest your awareness there.
- Now focus your awareness on your body.
- What feelings or emotions are being held in your body? Where in the body are you feeling them? Do they have a cool sensation or a warm sensation? Do they evoke a certain color?
- Let yourself simply be with these feelings. Fully attune to your body.

- Rest in the knowing that you can always "check in" with yourself.
- Let yourself simply feel the experience. And when you are ready, simply open your eyes.

Throughout the day, check in with yourself. Ask yourself, "What am I feeling now? Where in the body am I feeling it?" Be aware what difference, if any, this process makes on how attuned you are to yourself and others.

Chapter Ten

The Empaths: Empathy

Star Trek was one of my favorite TV series. Each episode was not only filled with adventures in far-off galaxies and life-and-death scenarios that threatened our favorite characters, but was laden with psychological metaphors and archetypal representations.

In one episode, Captain Kirk finds himself on a planet with a very unusual race of beings. These beings, all of whom were female and very attractive, were Empaths. These Empaths were subject to feeling whatever was present in the environment. If the environment was calm and serene, they too would be calm and serene. If the environment was hostile, they would feel agitated and uncomfortable. They felt and absorbed the energy of the person to whom they related. Needless to say, they were very sensitive beings, and they had a gift. Empaths could heal the sick. By placing their hands on the body of an individual, they could absorb the negative energy that caused the body to be sick and convert this energy into positive energy that could then heal the body.

Many of today's body workers use a similar approach, believing that they can infuse positive energy into the body to heal areas that are distressed.

As you might have already guessed, Kirk contracts a rare and deadly disease, a disease with no known cure. With great apprehension and total awareness that an attempt to save Kirk's life could cost the Empath her own life, she proceeds. She lays her hands on Kirk's body, and the negative energy from his body is absorbed into hers. Her body contorts in pain and anguish, and she is barely able to maintain contact with Kirk's body. Finally she loses consciousness, and both Empath and Kirk lie motionless on the floor. Then, the breath of life fills Kirk's body and he awakens. However, the Empath still remains unconscious. Kirk, in an overwhelming display of compassion, coddles the Empath's body, commanding her to live. He holds her tightly, rocking her back and forth, whispering in her ear, "Live." Finally, as if by divine intervention, her breath returns. She regains consciousness, and all is well.

Empathetic Connection

The empathic connection between mother and baby is perhaps the strongest experience two human beings can have. It resides outside of one's consciousness. It is a deeply felt, intuitive process. The body informs the mind. This is the opposite of the way adults most often become conscious of something: when the thinking mind informs the body. There seems to be an unfettered flow of energy between mother and infant, and this flow informs each person of the other's overall emotional and physical state.

As adults we may have similar experiences, particularly in romantic relationships. People who fall deeply in love will often report a "knowing" about the other that seems otherworldly. That is to say that they experience things about the other that are not derived through conventional means, such as being told something directly by the other person, or by observing something about the other person. This process of communication, this knowingness, has its origins from birth. Remember, at birth, we are simply feeling beings who can only define our world through our feelings. As a result, we are highly empathic and sensitive to the energy of our environment.

Empathic connection (empathy), or the experiencing of another's feelings, and attunement, or the state of being in harmony with another, are crucial underpinnings for emotional well-being. These processes not only contribute to our sense of well-being, but they establish an emotional mechanism we will use for the rest of our lives. Attunement and empathy allow us to connect deeply with other human beings and lay the foundation for us to experience compassion. They provide access to our intuitive self that informs us about our world. Often, when stress and anxiety interfere with our ability to attune to and empathically connect to other people, we feel isolated and disconnected from the world.

Unconditional Love

According to noted psychologist Carl Rogers, empathy and "unconditional positive regard" play a significant role in healthy human relations. Unconditional positive regard means that there is "blanket acceptance and support of a person regardless of what the person says or does."[27] Regardless of how a person behaves, their "being" is held in high regard, and their behavior is viewed as secondary to the essence of their being. It is this basic acceptance and support that is the foundation of the relationship. This practice was a major aspect of Rogerian psychotherapy.

Unconditional love encompasses unconditional positive regard. To love someone unconditionally means that you feel love and compassion for them simply because they are human. Your feeling toward the person does not depend on their behavior. A foundational feeling of love and acceptance of the person is at the core of the relationship. Most parents experience this towards their infants, particularly mothers. Communicating the experience of unconditional love is mainly nonverbal and becomes part of the empathetic connection between mother and child. It is a feeling held in the body, although certainly thoughts of this bond of love are present as well. This type of love experience also occurs in adult relationships.

When the primary caregiver loves the infant unconditionally, he or she establishes a context that supports the development of the infant's self-esteem. This context of unconditional love effectively communicates to the infant that they are worth loving. It further sets a standard that conveys what an intimate relationship can feel like. This, of course, is a very powerful relationship, one that communicates that the infant's welfare is paramount and takes precedence over the welfare of all others. It is what most of us desire in a relationship: the belief that our welfare comes before the welfare of the person to whom we are relating. If both people feel this way, an atmosphere of warmth, love, and connection can be maintained. But when this feeling is absent, or in fact the opposite feeling exists, when we feel our partners values themselves more than they value us, the relationship can begin to break down.

Unconditional love is not as easily established or developed as one would hope. It seems that this would be a natural process, particularly between parent and child. However, many variables can interfere with establishing a bond of this nature, many of which may not even be conscious. Any factor that moves an individual away from being emotionally open with regard to the relationship can interfere with the development of this bond.

For example, let's look at the relationship between mother and infant. If the mother is overly anxious about her mothering role, if the mother resents being a mother because of the enormity of the responsibility or the restriction of freedom that parenting imposes, if the mother is overly stressed or depressed, or if the mother is simply not very motherly, she can close down emotionally and cut off from her own feelings. Being cut off from her own feelings can interrupt her ability to be attuned to her baby which in turn can significantly interfere with the development of unconditional love. If this interference is consistent and ongoing, the relational pattern between mother and infant may not support the development of unconditional love.

Generally, every parent believes that he or she loves their child unconditionally, but often this is just an intellectual thought and not a deeply held feeling. This is not said to minimize the thoughts one has towards another. However, it is the feeling tone and the energy between individuals that ultimately conveys love.

Consider the following scenario I have frequently heard while working with couples in therapy. A wife complains that her husband "never" listens to her. She presents the following story. It's Sunday morning, and husband and wife sit down at the dining room table to have breakfast. He has his Sunday newspaper with him; she has her cup of coffee. She begins to talk to her husband about something while he begins to read his newspaper. "That's the problem!" she exclaims. "You never listen to me." He responds by saying, "I have heard every word you said." And, in fact, he then correctly repeats every word she said. So wherein lies the problem? The wife communicated a specific piece of information using her words (just like we have instructed our children to do: "Use your words!"). The husband has, in fact, heard every word spoken by the wife and can repeat verbatim every word communicated to him.

Something must be amiss, and that something is the feeling tone, the energy, between husband and wife. The wife doesn't "feel" heard by the husband. Yes, the husband can repeat every word she said, but the context of the experience is not one in which the wife feels regarded and acknowledged by the husband. The context is not one of feeling connected to each other. The words are being said and being received, but the energy between husband and wife, or lack thereof, doesn't support the wife's intention of this interaction. Her intention is to connect to her husband, and apparently this has not occurred for her. This is one of the most common themes that I have heard while working with couples.

So it is also with mother and infant. If the feeling tone is not there, the security provided through a relationship based on unconditional love will be minimized. This can impact the overall security and anxiety of the infant and impede the development of self-esteem. It can further hinder the emotional experience of the emerging child in regards to the child's love worthiness. Many of us actually feel unworthy of love. Essentially we feel either unlovable or not worthy enough to receive love. Much of the time it is because we haven't experienced a relationship in which we felt loved unconditionally.

When the Dalai Lama first came to the West, he was surprised to discover that some Westerners experience a feeling of self-loathing, or a general feeling of self-hatred and unworthiness. He remarked that this condition did not exist in his culture. He viewed this experience as being "incongruent" to the basic human desire to be happy and avoid suffering.

But there is good news. The developmental model we have been talking about is based on a process of *external validation*, that you're okay because I "say" so, and the "saying" is in the feeling tone conveyed and behavior displayed toward the infant by the mother or primary caretaker. Because a newborn is totally helpless, the baby is completely dependent on the environment for both physical and emotional survival. A baby does not have the internal resources (love) to comfort him or herself. They cannot *internally* validate themselves. They cannot say to themselves, "It's okay, you're okay." They need an outside source to provide this validation, and they need this validation to be consistently and continuously delivered. Through the care, attention, and love the mother or caretaker provides to the infant, the baby not only survives and thrives, but is validated.

This is the life of an infant. It is not, however, the life of an adult. Regardless of how little or how much we were validated and loved as a child, as adults we have the capacity to validate and love ourselves. But that pesky anxiety continually gets in our way. Perhaps if we had a better understanding of how self-esteem develops and how self-esteem combats anxiety, we could be more loving to ourselves.

Self-Esteem

Self-esteem is generally defined as one's overall appraisal of one's worth. Obviously, the higher one's self-esteem, the better. But this definition fails to name the essence of self-esteem, or what worth really is. Is worth a thought? Is it a feeling? Is it both? Since we apparently are not born with it and are unable to access it at birth, how do we acquire it?

Something that has "worth" has been defined as "something that has value." Value has been defined as "the quality that renders something desirable." So therefore, the concept of self-esteem suggests that it represents the degree to which one feels desirable and has value. But how does this happen? How does an infant who is totally dependent on the environment (mother or caretaker) develop a sense of value and desirability? The mother's attunement, empathetic connection, unconditional love, and her ability and willingness to validate the worth of her baby are all essential ingredients that contribute to self-esteem. However, there appears to be a specific process fundamental to the development of self-esteem.

As stated, the infant's world is the experience of either feeling calm or distressed. When the infant feels distressed, the infant calls out to signal the universe to help the infant return to a feeling of calm. Often the universe responds by way of the mother attending to her baby's needs and comforting her baby. This comforting allows the infant to transition from a distressed state to a calm state. This dance between mother and baby goes on countless times over many years.

Through this process the baby begins to associate the mother with comfort and security. The baby develops a feeling of what it is like to be in the presence of the mother. This feeling is a result, in part, of the soothing energy brought by the mother. Over repeated experiences of this interaction, the baby experiencing stress and the mother soothing her baby, the infant becomes able to conjure up this soothing feeling even when the mother is not immediately available. Some theorists have called this process "introjection," or internalizing the parent. This suggests that the baby actually internalizes (puts inside) the feeling tone of the mother. This process is not very different than what we do when we imagine something. When we imagine something, we often experience feelings that correspond to that which we imagine. If it is something wonderful, we may experience warm and joyful feelings, even though we are only imagining the experience. It doesn't exist in real time. It's not there. We are only imagining it. Unfortunately, the same type of response occurs when we imagine negative things, and the corresponding feelings of dread and worry may emerge. This process is essentially what the baby learns to do, and it is what we have all learned to do.

But now it gets a bit complicated. What exactly does the baby introject, and how much security will this introjection provide? The answer to this question is solely dependent on the individuals involved (mother and infant). An anxious, overprotective mother, relating to a low-threshold baby (one who is sensitive to the environment), will create a different introject or feeling tone than a calm, less-overbearing mother with a high-threshold baby (one who is less sensitive to the environment). And the introject itself is complex, with the baby introjecting all sorts of energy from the mother. The combinations of deciphering all of the mother's qualities and determining all of the baby's sensitivities are endless. However, what is important to understand is that through this process, self-esteem is born.

The fact that this helpless, dependent baby can begin to manage his or her own world, can begin to soothe itself and move itself from a distressed place to a calm place, is the origin of self-esteem. Relying on the "self" gives the "self" value. The foundation of self-esteem is the ability to self-soothe, to "say" to yourself "you're okay," to actually love yourself enough to feel safe. And, as said earlier, the "saying" starts as a feeling. It is an energetic process that feels like "you're okay," "you're good," "you can do this," "you're worthwhile," and "you have value."

Low-Keyedness

Margaret Mahler, an esteemed developmental psychologist, spent more than forty years observing infants in a controlled environment to observe infant development and has written at length about the process of child development. Starting in the 1950s, she filmed thousands of feet of film footage capturing the interactive patterns between mothers and infants, infants and strangers, etc. One such interactive pattern demonstrates well the process I have described above.

Mahler wrote about a process she called "low-keyedness." Low-keyedness is observed in infants when the infant is faced with an unfamiliar situation, i.e., faced with an encounter with a stranger when the infant is not in the arms of the mother. The infant's reaction is observed as "quieting," turning inward, eyes averted from the stranger and facing downward, with what appears to be a high level of concentration (sounds like meditation). Mahler's interpretation of this behavior was that the infant is concentrating inwardly in an attempt to capture the feeling the infant has when in the safety of the mother's arms. The infant is trying to self-soothe, trying to avoid moving from a calm state to an anxious state. By resonating with the feeling the infant has experienced when the mother has provided a sense of security, the infant hangs onto the state of calm.

However, once the external stimulus (the presence of the stranger) becomes too great (lasts too long), the infant cannot hold onto this security feeling any longer, and the infant will cry. The infant is returned to the mother to "recharge." That is to say that, once reunited with the mother, the infant regains the feeling of security from the mother and "fills the tank" (the internal feeling of security) to be used at the next situation that causes anxiety. Gradually "the tank" holds more and the infant uses less (i.e., the infant becomes more fuel efficient).

Love Yourself

Building a solid emotional foundation begins at home, and in this case, the home is ourselves. We must be kind to ourselves. We must forgive our imperfections and not judge ourselves as harshly as we have been taught by family and society. We must love ourselves unconditionally, simply based on the fact that we have been given this gift of life.

What does the flight attendant tell us at the beginning of every flight? "Put your own oxygen mask on first before assisting others." In the same manner, if we can't take care of ourselves, if we can't love ourselves, we are not going to be much good to somebody else.

How do we do that? The answer is by becoming aware and mindful of our thoughts and feelings. We must become aware of how we treat ourselves. We must choose to adopt an attitude of loving-kindness towards ourselves. We must fight the demons in our mind that criticize and tear us down and make us feel less than we are. We need to shut off the valve to that source of negative energy and open a valve to a positive energy source, the source of love present in our *true nature*. One way to do that is to calm the mind, which will calm the body and allow our true nature to surface. Mindfulness and meditation is an excellent vehicle to accomplish this very thing.

I have often asked clients the following question: "What is the first thing you have to do if you're trying to stop biting your nails?" Over the years, I have received many answers. But rarely have I received the correct answer, which is to be *aware* that your fingers are in your mouth. How can you stop biting your nails if you are not even aware that your fingers are in your mouth? Awareness is the key. It is the first ingredient that is necessary to make change. We must become aware of our thoughts and feelings that erode our sense of worth, our love of ourselves.

The Mindful Way: Loving-Kindness, Love Yourself

You can search the tenfold universe and not find a single being more worthy of loving-kindness than yourself.

Buddha

- Close your eyes. Begin mindful breathing. Be aware of breathing in and breathing out—just rest your awareness there.
- Now, very slowly, repeat the following three times:
  o May I be safe.
  o May I be well.
  o May I be at ease.
  o May I be happy.
  o May I love and honor myself.

Chapter Eleven

The Dumbo Effect:
Self-Confidence

In 1941, Walt Disney released a film entitled *Dumbo,* which would become a Disney classic. *Dumbo* is a story about a circus elephant. The story begins by introducing circus life and a pregnant elephant named Mrs. Jumbo. As the circus train roars to its next destination, Mrs. Jumbo waits patiently as the stork delivers baby after baby to the pregnant animals of the circus. Finally, long after all the other babies have been delivered, a stork finally arrives with Mrs. Jumbo's bundle of joy. Gently, the stork delivers the bundle, sings a happy birthday tune, and flies off, while the other elephants wait with excitement and anticipation. Mrs. Jumbo unwraps her newly arrived bundle to find a most adorable baby elephant. All the elephants are ecstatic and quickly ask what the baby will be named. Proudly, Mrs. Jumbo says, "Jumbo Jr." All are pleased. While being stroked by the mother's trunk, baby Jumbo Jr. sneezes. Out pop enormous ears. The ensemble of elephants is horrified. They taunt the baby elephant and, as part of their humiliating attack, rename him

"Dumbo." Finally Mrs. Jumbo retaliates and closes the hatch to their stall, sending it cascading down on their heads. Both momma and baby are shunned by the other elephants.

Not long after this incident, an even more troubling incident occurs. After the Big Tent has been set up, the patrons are allowed entry to view the animals prior to the show. A group of teenagers spot Dumbo and start taunting Dumbo about his ears and making fun of him. Outraged, Dumbo's mother reacts and protects her baby by shooting peanuts at the teenagers, chasing them from Dumbo. A ruckus breaks out, and eventually the Big Tent comes tumbling down. Mrs. Jumbo is hauled away and locked up in a railway car with the words "Mad Elephant" painted on the boxcar. Baby Dumbo is left all alone to fend for himself, the other elephants ignoring his presence.

A little mouse witnesses the behavior of the elephants towards Dumbo and takes pity on him. He quickly befriends Dumbo and castigates the other elephants for their behavior. The mouse, aware of Dumbo's sadness, attempts to cheer him up and tells Dumbo that he has arranged a meeting with Dumbo's mother and that she is waiting for him. Off they go. They find the boxcar where Mrs. Jumbo is jailed, and the mouse calls out to her and informs her that she has a visitor. Chained inside the boxcar, only Mrs. Jumbo's long trunk can reach through the boxcar's bars, enabling her to stroke and caress Dumbo.

Eventually it is time to leave, and Dumbo and his little mouse friend wander off. Dumbo suddenly develops a case of hiccups. The mouse directs Dumbo to a bucket filled with water. However, unbeknownst to him, an open bottle of alcohol has fallen into the bucket. Soon both Dumbo and the mouse are very drunk and begin hallucinating. This experience ends with both mouse and elephant waking up the following morning in a tree. As they sit up in their tree, flabbergasted as to how they got up there, they are greeted by a flock of crows. The crows are laughing at their predicament and break out in song, singing, "I've seen a house fly. I've seen a shoe fly. But I ain't never seen an elephant fly." The mouse realizes that the only way they could have gotten up into that tree is if Dumbo had flown them up there. He begins to explain this reality to Dumbo and assures Dumbo that he can fly them out of the tree. But Dumbo is very resistant to this idea. Finally, the mouse grabs a feather from a crow and tells Dumbo that it's a magic feather. He assures Dumbo that as long as Dumbo has the magic feather, Dumbo can fly. He eventually cajoles Dumbo into taking the risk and launching them out of the tree. At first Dumbo heads straight for the ground, but the mouse encourages Dumbo that he can fly—and fly he does.

Meanwhile, the circus, not knowing what to do with Dumbo, does the unconscionable. They make Dumbo a clown. This outrages the other elephants. Dressed as a clown, Dumbo's role is to jump from a burning building into a net held by clowns dressed as firemen. Underneath the net is a bucket of water in which Dumbo would plunge, creating a big splash and lots of laughs. Dumbo, outfitted as a clown, sits high above the Big Tent arena, perched on a platform atop the burning building, awaiting his cue to jump. His friend the mouse, tucked into his hat, calmly talks to Dumbo to assure him that everything will be all right. "You got the magic feather?" he asks, as Dumbo clutches the feather in his trunk. Finally, it is time for Dumbo to jump. With great apprehension and a poke from behind, Dumbo jumps. Heading straight into the ground, the mouse encourages Dumbo to have faith in the magic feather and fly. Just as it seems that he would, the velocity of Dumbo's speed rips the magic feather from Dumbo's trunk. Dumbo is left in a free fall as the mouse, terrified, shouts into his ear, "It was a gag. The magic feather was a gag. Fly, Dumbo! You can fly." Just as Dumbo is about to hit the ground, he turns up his head, spreads out his ears, and takes flight. He flies throughout the Big Tent, harassing the clowns and thrilling the patrons.

Dumbo became the star of the circus. He was given his own wagon and reunited with his mother, and he, his mother, and his beloved friend the mouse lived like kings.

Discrimination and Empathy

There is much to learn from this story. This is a story about humiliation, abandonment, isolation, self-confidence, and, whether intended or not, racism. Pretty nice kids' story! Let's analyze the story and see how it might fit into some of the things we have already discussed.

Mrs. Jumbo, whose mate is never mentioned or shown in the film, is expecting a baby. Within the elephant community, there is great excitement about the impending birth. All are joyous that a newborn elephant will be joining their ranks. The onlooking elephants greet the delivering stork with great pride. Once the baby elephant has been delivered to Mrs. Jumbo, all cannot wait to get their first glimpse of the new arrival. When the baby is finally revealed, all are delighted. But then something happens. Dumbo's ears unfurl and his true identity is discovered. The elephant community reacts with disgust; denigrates the baby elephant by changing his given name to Dumbo, a derogatory name; and vows not to accept him as a member of their community.

A side note about elephants: Asian elephants have much smaller ears than their African counterparts and are said to be more intelligent than African elephants. By virtue of his ears, Dumbo clearly is an African elephant and, by virtue of his mother being an Asian elephant, a product of a "mixed" union. Remember, this film was made in 1941, a time when racial intolerance was the norm.

The scene prior to Dumbo's arrival, which I have not presented, was filled with racial overtones. The scene shows the construction of the Big Tent taking place during a huge thunder and lightning storm. All of the workers setting up the Big Tent in the storm are black. They are working in nearly impossible conditions, singing a song that describes them as "working day and night, can't read or write, spending their money as soon as they get it, but happy with their lot in life."

Whether Dumbo is a victim of racial discrimination or not, he is clearly a victim of discrimination. By virtue of his appearance, he has been scorned and humiliated. His mother, as a result of her protecting behavior towards her child, has been hauled off to jail, leaving Dumbo abandoned and "without a friend in the world." Dumbo is scared, lonely, and depressed, a response we would expect from anyone who had suffered such a trauma. He is made to be a clown, a station in life that is far below the dignity of his "species." He is generally dismissed and faces a continuous barrage of ridicule.

Then something happens to Dumbo. One kind soul, in the body of a mouse, takes pity and befriends Dumbo. It seems clear that this mouse has an empathetic understanding regarding the feelings Dumbo is experiencing. As a result of witnessing how Dumbo has been treated by his fellow pachyderms, this tiny little mouse is filled with compassion and responds by providing Dumbo with love and kindness. The mouse runs through the elephant's encampment, scaring these mighty beasts and chastising their behavior. "You ought to be ashamed of yourselves, picking on a poor defenseless..." he shouts. "Come on, Dumbo," he softly commands, and leads Dumbo away from the humiliating assemblage. He then proceeds to "pump Dumbo up." He assures him that everything will be okay and, in an attempt to lift Dumbo's spirits, he does the one thing he intuitively knows will work. He takes Dumbo to visit his imprisoned mother. Empathy guided this "lowly" little mouse to embrace Dumbo's plight and provide Dumbo with the love and support needed to help him through this difficult situation. We could all learn a lot from this mouse.

Ridicule and Humiliation

We have all experienced ridicule and humiliation. Whether it was from a teacher in front of the class commenting on our poor performance or a family member in our own home, ridicule and humiliation are feelings we are all familiar with. Have you ever wondered why parents criticize or even humiliate their own children? Is it because they are mean spirited? For some this may be the reason, but for most it is not. Criticism and humiliation are often delivered as a means to motivate. Parents witness a behavior that they do not like and want their children to behave differently. Instead of creating a situation in which they can positively reinforce a new behavior, they will often criticize the "old" behavior. Take, for example, the scenario of a child watching television instead of doing their homework. This aggravates the parent, and as a result of the aggravation, the parent says, "You're just a lazy good-for-nothing." Whether or not it is obvious, this statement is made with the intention of motivating the child to actually do their homework. Unfortunately, this very common scenario is not an effective method to accomplish the goal of motivating the child to do homework. All this statement does is support the idea that the child is lazy, and if the child believes that he is lazy, then lazy he will be. We know that negative reinforcement and punishment are poor motivators to elicit new behavior.

Identification with the Aggressor

In the field of psychology, the concept known as "identification with the aggressor" relates directly to the discussion at hand and to Dumbo's plight. This concept suggests that our identity, or how we think and feel about ourselves, is significantly influenced by how the authority figure (the aggressor) within a system views us. It further states that we tend to identify with the values held by that authority figure. If the authority figure holds a negative view towards us, we are likely to identify with this view. If the authority figure has a negative value system, such as "women are inferior to men," then we tend to adopt this value system. This is experienced on an unconscious level, as if we simply absorb these beliefs. In extreme situations, this process can be very damaging. Victims of abuse have often identified with the values their abusers held towards them. Jews held in concentration camps during World War II often assumed the devaluing opinions of their captors.

From a rational vantage point, this process can be understood in the following way. The authority figure represents the high-status holder. Therefore, the opinion of the high-status holder is most valued. If the high-status holder believes that you are worthless, and you are in a situation in which you are dependent and impressionable (such as childhood), then you are likely to feel worthless.

We want to trust the high-status holder. Trusting the high-status holder gives us a sense of security in the world. We desperately want to trust the opinions of our parents, our teachers, and our political, religious, and community leaders, even when their opinions may negatively affect our own opinions of ourselves. Imagine how Dumbo felt about himself.

Believe in Yourself

Obviously, being exposed to a significantly negative view of oneself can leave us feeling anxious, depressed, and insecure. Our self-confidence is undermined when our world tells us that we are "less than." Dumbo was an emotional wreck. The high-status holders constantly reinforced Dumbo's worthlessness. However, through the caring and support of another, through the reassurance from his friend the mouse that he was okay, Dumbo emerges as the star that he is.

There was a little trickery in this relationship, but nothing outside the ordinary. After all, the mouse did convince Dumbo that as long as he had the magic feather, he could fly. How is this much different than a toddler who holds tightly to their security blanket? Does the blanket truly have magical powers that allow the child to feel secure? Perhaps in the mind of the child it does, but we know differently.

In fact, a security blanket, or any other significant transitional object, is an interesting phenomenon. The object does allow the child to feel more secure. Why does this happen? The answer is that the object has been imbued with the "loving energy" of the primary caretaker (mother). The object, on an unconscious level, represents the protective, supportive, loving qualities of the primary caretaker. It's as if the mother is right there with the child, holding the child in a protective embrace. Eventually, these qualities are introjected into the child. They reside in the emotional cavern of the child and are available to the child on an ongoing basis without the need of the transitional object. These feelings of security live within the child and allow the child to deal with situations in the child's world that may produce fear and anxiety. If the situation is too fearful, the child will seek out the support and comfort of the caretaker. Through the repetition of this dance, the child builds a still-greater sense of internal security.

Dumbo's self-reliance came rather quickly. As he jumped from the platform situated high atop the Big Tent, his magic feather was dislodged. Fear surged through his body. But there was a voice, similar to our internal voice, speaking to him: his friend, the mouse. The mouse kept encouraging Dumbo that he could fly. He kept reiterating that the magic feather was a gag (a transitional object of sorts) and that Dumbo had it in him to fly. And fly he did. Perhaps the moral of this story is that when we believe in ourselves, we can reach amazing heights.

Years ago I attended a conference that hosted the Dalai Lama. It was my first time to see the Dalai Lama, and I was excited to hear about his insights on life. After a brief talk, he invited the audience to ask questions. One question posed to him was, "What is the most important thing in life?" I thought that this question was rather vague and that the Dalai Lama would certainly reply by commenting on our need to be compassionate, or our need to seek a spiritual life. However, he surprised me. He said, "You must believe in yourself. This is the most important thing in life." I have contemplated that statement for many decades. And when I think of Dumbo's plight, I have a better understanding of the importance of the Dalai Lama's statement.

The Mindful Way: Believe in Yourself

- Close your eyes. Begin mindful breathing. Be aware of breathing in and breathing out—just rest your awareness there.
- Now let your awareness shift to the way you see yourself. Examine how you perceive your strengths and weaknesses.
- Concentrate on your weaknesses.

- *Recognize* in what ways you maintain a limiting view of yourself.
- *Accept* that this is a view that you hold.
- *Investigate* why you hold these views.
- *Non-identify* with these views. Say to yourself, "These views are only thoughts."
- Now transform these perceived weaknesses into strengths. Imagine how they can serve you in a positive way.
- Just sit with this experience.
- Now imagine yourself utilizing these newly acquired strengths in your life. What does this look like? How does this feel? Where in your body do you feel this experience?
- Now say to yourself, "I believe in me. I have confidence in myself." Repeat this for as long as you need.
- When you are ready, open your eyes.

Chapter Twelve

The Long Island Sound Story: Dependency

When I was nineteen years old, on a cold April 1 day, my older brother (eight years older) and I took a small aluminum boat, outfitted with an outboard motor, and went fishing in Long Island Sound. That year New York had a very prolonged, cold winter, and as a result, the water temperature was very cold. It was late in the day, and after a few hours of catching nothing, we "hit" a school of flounder. However, just as we located this school of fish, a squall came up and started drenching us. The sea became turbulent. The wind was gushing, and conditions were rapidly deteriorating. I looked down at my feet, which were now sitting in about a half of a foot of sea water, and noticed that the flounder we had caught and placed in a bucket were swimming around my feet. "Hey, who let the flounder out?" I exclaimed, just as a wave came over the bow of the boat and dropped the boat out from under us.

There we sat, legs bent as if sitting on the boat's bench, bobbing in the sea, with no boat under us. It took a moment to realize what had occurred, and in moments like these, time takes on another dimension. We were nearly a mile from shore. The water temperature was in the high fifty-degree range at best. We were heavily clothed, with boots on our feet: not ideal clothing for swimming.

What do you suppose my immediate reaction was? Out of habit, I looked toward my older brother with one thought in mind, "My brother will save me," only to hear the words from him that I will remember for the rest of my life: "Swim for your life." Are you kidding me? Swim for my life? What are you talking about? Then it hit me. My brother was not going to rescue me. He would be lucky if he was able to rescue himself. At that very moment, my dependency on my brother, a brother whom I had always looked to for help, shifted forever. I got it. I swam for my life.

It took only seconds before my brother and I lost sight of each other. The waves were high and the light was darkening. In an effort to preserve energy, I was soon on my back, doing the backstroke. Suddenly, I heard a voice: "This way, swim this way," it called. I turned toward the voice and saw something that I will never forget and something that I couldn't comprehend at the time. There stood my brother on top of the sea calling out to me. This image made no sense to me. He literally stood on top of the water. I didn't know if I was having a religious experience.

I swam towards him as hard as I could, expending the last bit of energy I had. As I came upon him, he reached down and pulled me up on top of a huge boulder that was still submerged under the water. The tide was going out, and although the boulder was still under water, we could perch ourselves on it, clinging to life. It took nearly two more hours before help arrived.

First the helicopter came, but the wind was too fierce to attempt a rescue. Eventually, with the helicopter circling and shining a floodlight on our position, a small rowboat was launched from shore, heading to our rock. By now our boulder stood six feet above the sea, so it was no easy task navigating from the rock to the boat. We both made it safely.

Dependency

Dependency is relying on someone or something else to have your needs met, regardless of what those needs might be. If I go to the grocery store to buy some food, I am dependent on that store to have the food I need to buy. If I plant a garden to provide me with my own food, then I will not be dependent on the grocery store; however, I will be dependent on other variables, such as the weather, the soil conditions, etc. As you can see, it is nearly impossible to be completely independent.

Most of the time, being less reliant on others and being more self-reliant reduces anxiety, because we have effectively eliminated a step that can cause anxiety. The step that is eliminated is the act of needing something from someone or something, which by definition is outside of our control. When in a dependent situation, we hope that whomever or whatever we are dependent upon will deliver what we need. However, being in a dependent position can cause anxiety. The magnitude of our anxiety can be influenced by the significance of what we are dependent on. For example, if we have interviewed for a job that can impact our life, we may have much greater anxiety while awaiting the decision of the interviewer than if we are driving to our local market to buy a specific food item.

Dependency can be habitual. Once oriented in the world as a dependent being, it can become difficult to break the habit and rely on yourself. Being in an environment that supports a high degree of dependency can actually lead to helplessness. Consider the child who has been raised in an environment in which her caretakers did everything for her, including making even minor decisions, such as what she will eat when in a restaurant. In extreme situations, this can lead to what is known as a "dependent personality." These are adults who are extremely dependent on others to make decisions for them, and if forced to make their own they become highly anxious. Many of us have some degree of this dynamic. As you can see from my Long Island Sound experience, my first impulse when faced with this life-threatening situation was to turn to my older brother for help rather than relying immediately on myself. However, as a result of this experience and my ability to rely heavily on myself, my dependency on my brother and my dependency in general seemed to change.

Sometimes people are so anxious about being dependent on others they actually remove themselves from society so they don't have to encounter situations of dependency, such as hermits, or people who act as if they don't need anyone. They construct a lifestyle that depends very little on others. However, this is a response to an extreme fear of, or an anxiety fostered by, dependency, and in this situation their self-reliance doesn't actually enhance their self-esteem. This is similar to putting the padlock on the closet door to deal with the ghost, as discussed in chapter 9. In this situation, self-reliance is the padlock. As stated earlier, it is emotional self-reliance (the ability to calm oneself) and not simply physical self-reliance (the ability to manage one's outside environment) that leads to a sense of well-being.

We are all dependent on one another in one way or the other. Marriage, for example, is a dependent relationship. It is a partnership. "I will do this, and you will do that, and together we will accomplish our goals or tasks." In fact, we are all interconnected and, as a result, dependent on each other and our environment for our survival. Maintaining an appropriate degree of dependency and being aware of our dependencies in our lives can contribute to our emotional well-being. When we are attuned to ourselves and our environment, we can make better decisions regarding when we need to be dependent and on whom, or what, we will depend.

Self-Reliance and Autonomy

Self-reliance has been defined as "reliance on oneself or one's own powers and resources."

I love this definition: one's own powers and resources. It makes it sound rather mystical. For me, it brings up images of Mickey Mouse in the Disney film *Fantasia*, in the piece entitled "The Sorcerer's

Apprentice." Mickey is a young apprentice to an all-powerful sorcerer. He has yet to master the powers of sorcery. Left to do chores while the sorcerer leaves, Mickey decides to use his undisciplined powers and resources and enchants a broom to do his bidding: carrying water. It doesn't take long for the broom to become many brooms and run rampant. As a consequence, the place becomes flooded, and Mickey finds himself in a rather serious and potentially dangerous situation. Of course, the sorcerer returns and alleviates the problem, saves Mickey, and sternly chastises him for his behavior.

Autonomy is an ancient Greek word meaning "one who gives oneself his own law." It is synonomous with self-reliance. As Mickey somewhat exemplifies, developing autonomy takes time and maturity. Unlike other animals, we human beings are not able to govern ourselves at birth. In fact, given the nature of most of the world's political systems, there appears to be a belief that we are never able to fully govern ourselves. Anarchy, or the absence of a governing body designed to regulate our behavior, is seen as a negative state of existence, a society inundated with political and social disorder. However, just imagine if we were emotionally mature enough to self-regulate. Imagine that each of us is an autonomous human being, and based on an internal sense of security and safety, we could govern ourselves in a manner that does no harm to others and in fact supports the existence of our fellow human beings.

Immanuel Kant, the eighteenth-century philosopher, maintained that one ought to think autonomously, free of the dictates of external authority. He believed that we do have the capacity to self-govern and that we should exist as independent entities.

Dependency and Autonomy Integrated

Drs. Robert Bornstein and Mary Languirand address the relationship between dependency and autonomy in their book, *Healthy Dependency*. They describe healthy dependency as "leaning on others without losing yourself." They state the following:

There is a healthy middle ground between rigid independence and unhealthy overdependence. Healthy dependency is the ability to blend intimacy and autonomy, lean on others while maintaining a strong sense of self, and feel good (not guilty) about asking for help when you need it. Healthy dependency means depending on people without becoming dependent on them. It means trusting people enough to open up and be vulnerable; yet having the self confidence you need to survive those inevitable relationship conflicts that everyone experiences at one time or another.[28]

In their research they found that the happiest, most-satisfied, well-adjusted people were ones that balanced dependency with autonomy, self-confidence, and trust. These people had the ability to lean on others without feeling guilty, weak, or ashamed.

So if blending dependency with autonomy is healthy, when is dependency unhealthy? The core problem is illuminated when we talk about "emotional dependence," not just dependence, which we will do in the next chapter.

The Mindful Way: Loving-Kindness and the Unnoticed People in Your Life

Think of the dependent relationships you maintain in your life. Think of all the people who help support your existence, including the people we tend not to give much notice, such as the grocery store cashier, or the bank teller, or a sanitation worker.

- Close your eyes. Begin mindful breathing. Be aware of breathing in and breathing out—just rest your awareness there.

- Now imagine a person who is helpful or who has been kind to you, a person who tends to reside in the background of your life. Slowly repeat the following three times:
  - ○ May you be safe.
  - ○ May you be well.
  - ○ May you be at ease.
  - ○ May you be happy.
  - ○ May you love and honor yourself.
- The next time you encounter this person, see if this exercise changes your interaction.

Chapter Thirteen

The Missing Piece Meets the Big O: Emotional Dependency

The American author Shel Silverstein wrote a lovely book entitled *The Missing Piece Meets the Big O*.[29] This book illustrates, both figuratively and literally, the concepts of autonomy, emotional dependence, and the need to be externally validated through a relationship.

The story begins with a pie-slice-shaped object called the "Missing Piece." The Missing Piece is very sad because he doesn't feel complete, and he is desperately seeking his counterpart to fit into so he will feel whole and fulfilled. His journey takes him across the path of many objects that are circular in nature and are also missing a piece, as would a pie with a slice missing. As he encounters each circular object, he explains his situation and then proceeds to try and fit himself into them to make a complete circle. Every attempt fails. Either he is too big, or too wide, or too small.

Finally the Missing Piece seems to find his match. He leaps into the object, and sure enough, he fits perfectly: together they form a complete

151

circle. The Missing Piece feels pure delight because now he feels whole. The newly formed circle goes along its merry way. But then something begins to occur. The Missing Piece begins to grow. Try as he might to stop this process, he can't. Eventually he grows too big and pops out of the circle. Once again he is all alone and feels unwhole.

As the Missing Piece sits despondently at the side of the curb, an unusual object approaches. The Missing Piece has never seen an object like this before. This object, named the Big O, is a perfectly formed circle. The Big O looks down at the Missing Piece and asks, "Why are you so sad?" The Missing Piece looks up at the Big O and explains his dilemma and the journey he has undertaken to resolve his problem. The Big O says, "That's too bad. I can't really help you with that, but if you would like to come along with me, you are welcome." The Missing Piece, feeling lonely and out of options, decides to travel along with the Big O. Off they go.

As we witness the two of them traveling side by side, we begin to notice yet another transformation in the Missing Piece. Over time, through the motion of traveling beside the Big O but not as part of the Big O, a motion that requires the Missing Piece to roll end over end, the pie-slice shape of the Missing Piece begins to round, until he too becomes a perfect circle.

Emotional Dependence

Emotional dependence occurs when one person is dependent on another person to make them feel okay about themselves. The less emotionally dependent we are in our relationships, the more of ourselves we can actually bring into the relationship.

The process of emotional dependence can be rather complex, most likely because the process is often not conscious. In other words, two people enter into a relationship with a covert arrangement between them. Each person in the relationship is required to validate the worth of the other. As long as this "contract" is fulfilled, each person is happy. But the moment either party stops delivering, the negative feelings begin. Many marriages and couple relationships are based on this process.

Just as there is a relationship between autonomy and anxiety, there also appears to be a relationship between autonomy and emotional dependence. Generally, the more autonomous an individual, the less emotionally dependent they seem to be.

This reliance on another person to provide a sense of well-being and self-worth is contrary to what has been described previously as self-esteem. Remember, self-esteem develops as a result of external validation provided by the mother and other caretakers, but it is an intrinsic experience. It is an *internal* process in which a person feels good about themselves, feeling a sense of worth and value. Emotional dependency is based on an external validation in which a person looks to the outside world (their primary relationship) for validation of themselves. This is not to suggest that there is necessarily anything wrong with external validation. Most of us enjoy being validated by other people, and, in fact, being in a validating environment is good for us. It can support and bolster our positive feelings about ourselves. It can even help someone who has low-esteem develop higher esteem in a similar fashion as the process that occurs in infancy. However, each member of an emotionally dependent relationship is *attached* to the validation provided through the relationship, and when the validation is no longer forthcoming, their esteem plummets.

Internal Validation

Consider the following question. What is the difference between a reptile and a mammal? A primary answer to this question is that a reptile is a cold-blooded animal, while a mammal is a warm-blooded animal. What this means is that the body temperature of a reptile fluctuates based on the temperature of their environment. A reptile's body temperature decreases when it's cold outside and increases when it's warm outside. Its body temperature is dependent on the external world. On the other hand, mammals have a constant body temperature.

Their body temperature does not fluctuate based on the temperature of their environment. Their body temperature is constant and internally regulated. Usually any fluctuation in body temperature, albeit small, is a result of some insult or trauma to the body, such as a virus or bacteria.

This comparison is analogous to the difference between someone whose self-worth is dependent on external validation (I hate to call them cold blooded, but you get the point), contrasted with someone whose self-worth is internally validated (warm blooded) and not subject to significant fluctuations based on external factors.

What is internal validation? Let's ponder the question. I decided to research this term and find the most accurate definition, and then present this definition accordingly. I began first by researching on the Internet, only to find numerous articles relating to internal validation and research methods. Even when I researched the term "emotional internal validation," the definitions were not germane to this discussion. So instead I turned to my vast library of psychology texts. I looked through all of my child development, emotional development, and life-span development books, and I was surprised to find no specific references to internal validation. I found this to be most puzzling, particularly because the concept of internal validation is one of the most substantial concepts related to emotional well-being.

Internal validation is the ability of an individual to *validate* themselves, or to "confirm," "approve," "authenticate," "substantiate," or "ascertain the truth," *internally,* or "from within." It is the ability to *know* without needing approval or confirmation from the outside world. In essence, it is the process of "approving" of oneself, and it is the essential ingredient of high self-esteem. It is self-love. It is the experience of knowing that you are "okay" without needing an external factor to make you feel "okay," be it a job, a relationship, social status, education level, or material possessions. It is the quintessential process that promotes emotional well-being and contributes to equanimity: the emotional state of calmness, stability, and composure, even in the face of stress and tension.

Certain personality types have a very difficult time experiencing internal validation. They are oriented to seek validation and self-worth from the outside world. For some (often male), their self-worth is measured by their successes: how much money they make, how high their job status is, how affluent their neighborhood, and how beautiful their spouse. For others (often female), their self-worth is measured by their primary relationship and whether they have constructed the family life and social network they have always dreamed of. Of course, this is a fairly traditional view. However, given that we live in a world of impermanence, all of these externally validating trappings can vanish. And when this occurs, it can leave those of us who are attached to these "things" for a sense of self-worth feeling extremely vulnerable and quite worthless.

Consider what has been going on across America since the early 2000s. Since the economic collapse, people have been losing their jobs and their homes. The increase in stress has often led to the demise of their primary relationship. Not only does the individual experience these losses as a loss of security, they also feel shame and diminished self-worth. When our self-worth is attached to an externally validating "object," it will always be subject to fluctuations.

When we are able to experience internal validation in the throes of distress, we are more likely to say, "It will be all right. It's only money," or "It's only a job." We become less attached to the objects in our world and less reliant on them for our sense of self-worth. We may experience less anxiety when our external world begins to crumble, or when we do, we tend to recover from our pain and anxiety more quickly. As mentioned earlier, we are more emotionally resilient.

The Puddle

Imagine that you are at the beach. You walk down to the water's edge and notice a blue plastic pail, the type a child would use to play at the beach. You bend down, pick up the pail, and decide to make a puddle. Barefooted, you proceed into the water, bending over to dip the pail into the ocean and fill it with seawater. You then back out of the water and walk a few feet away from the water's edge, where the sand is dry and not impacted by the ocean's waves. You dump the water from the pail directly onto the sand. The force of the water hitting the sand makes an impression in the sand that immediately fills up with the water you have just poured. As a result of your effort, a small puddle has formed. However, within seconds, the puddle begins to drain as it is absorbed into the dry sand. Unconcerned, you rush back to the water, fill the pail again, run back to the now wet spot in the sand and pour the water out again. This time, instead of admiring your work, you quickly turn, race back to the water, fill the pail, and run back to the newly formed puddle and fill it with the water from the pail. You do this over and over again until you have before you a substantial puddle.

You take a break, sit down next to your newly created puddle, and admire your work. But it's not long before you notice that your puddle is dwindling, once again being absorbed into the sand. Up you jump, race back to the water, pail in hand, and start the entire ritual over again. Again and again you repeat this dance. Time and time again you are faced with the same results: you create a puddle in the sand by constantly feeding it water, but once you stop your puddle disappears. Defeated, you put the pail down beside the disappearing puddle and walk away.

Let's examine this scenario. You want a puddle. You provide the necessary ingredient, water, to make a puddle. You continually pour water into the sand to create the puddle. But once you stop feeding the puddle, the puddle disappears and you're left simply with a wet spot. Wherein lies the problem? Is it the water you are using? Perhaps it is your pouring technique. Obviously, it's neither of these issues. So it must be the sand. But what is it about the sand? Is the sand too soft, or too dry, or too coarse, or too fine? None of these conditions really matter much. What does matter, however, is the *foundation* of the sand. And what we know about sand on a beach is that there isn't much of a foundation. Certainly if you were to dig deeply enough and remove the top layers of sand, you would find that the consistency of the sand, due to moisture that has been entrapped, was more densely compacted. However, even at this level, the base is porous and therefore not a solid foundation. Unless you can continually pour water into your puddle, your puddle will not hold the water you have given it. Poor puddle.

By analogy, emotionally dependent relationships attempt to do the same thing. Emotionally dependent relationships try to "water" each other to create a "puddle" of self-worth in each other. But if there is little to no emotional foundation within the individuals in this relationship, all the praise and support given in the relationship is like pouring water into the sand. You may get a puddle, but eventually that puddle will disappear.

The Emotionally Dependent Relationship

Any relationship which is based on emotional or any other dependency has a likelihood of restricting the relationship. Think about the common relationship an individual has with their boss. By definition, this relationship has a high degree of dependency. We need our job. Our boss can terminate our employment. Therefore, we are in a dependent relationship. This relationship may not necessarily involve emotional dependency, though often it does. Because we perceive ourselves as being in a relationship with a degree of risk (the termination of the relationship), we often modify our behavior in the relationship. For example, rarely do people who believe themselves to be in a subordinate role in a relationship (an employee with an employer) "speak their mind" fully and share how they may actually feel. They are often concerned about saying anything that is overly critical or negative. They tend to be "nice" to their employer to mitigate the risk of upsetting the boss and losing their job.

To illustrate this point, consider the following question: "Is it more likely for a commercial airliner to crash when it is being flown by the captain of the plane, or flown by the first officer?" Malcolm Gladwell explores this very issue in his book *Outliers*. Gladwell explains that most commercial airplanes are piloted by a captain and a first officer, who share the responsibility of flying the plane. This means that at times the captain is at the controls, and the first officer's responsibility is to observe and be cognizant of how things are going. Other times the first officer is flying the plane, and it's the captain's responsibility to watch over things. By definition the captain is the senior officer, with more experience and flying time than the first officer.

Is it more likely for a commercial airliner to crash while being flown by the more experienced captain or by the less experienced first officer? Common sense would lead us to believe that it would be the less experienced first officer. However, several decades of data regarding commercial airline crashes tell us that the majority of crashes happened while the airplane was piloted by the captain.

How can we make sense of this information, and what does it have to do with what we have discussed? The answer lies in a term known as "mitigated speech." Mitigated speech is a linguistic term used to describe deferential or indirect speech, or as Gladwell put it, "any attempt to downplay or sugarcoat the meaning of what is being said."[30] We mitigate our speech by being polite, or by not directly saying what we need to say. This often occurs when we relate to authority. This behavior is also a classic example of restricting our behavior in a relationship.

Even in the face of extreme imminent danger, even as the airplane was descending towards a crash, many first officers were unwilling to directly tell their superior officer, the captain at the controls, that they were messing up. Think about the implications of this information. Even when faced with a high probability of a crash, and therefore their passengers' deaths as well as their own, these first officers would literally rather die than offend their captain. How ingrained does this social construct have to be to actually risk death rather than speaking up? Well, that's easy to answer. Extremely ingrained! And to varying degrees, it is ingrained in most of us.

Marriages and couple relationships can operate in the same manner. Because of the emotionally dependent nature of the relationship, either individual may restrict their behavior in an attempt to maximize the security of the relationship and get their emotional needs met.

The Pink Couch

Let me tell you the story of the pink couch. Years ago, newly married and after buying our house, my wife and I decided that we had better buy some furniture for the house. Having spent most of our money purchasing the house, there was very little money left to furnish it. I had noticed that there was a huge furniture liquidation sale that was being held in the parking lot of the Oakland Coliseum, where the Oakland A's baseball team played. I suggested that we could probably get some great deals on furniture, and off we went.

Walking through this giant parking lot filled with furniture, I noticed a couch. The couch was a pink, three-piece, sectional couch. I thought a sectional couch could work nicely in the living room, situated around the fireplace. The price was very reasonable. As we approached the seller, I said to my wife, "Wouldn't that look great in the living room?" to which she demurely replied, "Yes." So I made the deal and arranged to have the couch delivered later that same day. Of course, all sales were final.

We finished our shopping, buying a few smaller items, and went home to await the arrival of our newly purchased couch. Soon the delivery truck pulled up to our house, unloaded the couch, and began the descent down to our entryway (we live on a hillside). "Boy, I'm glad I don't have to carry that thing," I said to myself. They placed it exactly where I had imagined it would go, and left. I stood staring at the couch. Finally I said, "I hate it," to which my wife responded, "I thought so." I paused, collecting my thoughts, trying to process what had just occurred. "What did you say?" I asked my wife. She repeated her statement, and she went on to explain that she hadn't liked the couch from the start. "What?" I exclaimed. "Well," she said, "I didn't want to hurt your feelings. You seemed to like it." That was it. I basically lost it and told her to never do that again. I explained that we have an equal partnership, and I need to be confident that she will give me her input on major decisions, as will I do for her.

Somehow I managed to convince the furniture company to let me exchange the couch for other furniture. Of course, I had to lug the thing up the stairs and rent a truck to bring it back. However, in the end, it was a valuable lesson for both of us, one that effectively resolved this type of communication between us and provided me with a story that I have used with my clients for many years.

Interestingly, I recently used this story during a couples' workshop I was conducting. The couples in attendance were from the Midwest, and I was surprised at their reactions. Virtually each of the couples said that they would never disagree with their spouse in front of a salesperson. They said that they would rather buy an ugly couch than *shame* their spouse. I found it very enlightening to realize that they believed voicing an opposing opinion in front of a neutral, unknown party would be shaming behavior. This insight led to some very interesting dialogue within the group.

Abusive Relationships

An extreme version of a type of relationship that reflects these dynamics is the abusive relationship. Despite the abuse, the abused continues not only to stay in the relationship, but to modify behavior to ensure the continuation of the relationship. Unfortunately, the abuse has little to do with the other person's behavior and more to do with the emotional dysfunctionality of the abuser.

Many years ago, I recall seeing a particular movie scene that depicted this dynamic. The main character was an alcoholic father who intermittently verbally and physically abused his family. His preferred target was his teenage daughter. One evening the daughter requests permission from her father to attend a friend's birthday party. Her father grants permission and demands that she returns home no later than 11 p.m.

During the daughter's absence from the house, the father proceeds to get drunk and pass out on the living room sofa. Upon the daughter's return, at the designated 11 p.m. curfew, the daughter quietly (modified behavior) attempts to slip through the living room on her way to her bedroom and avoid an encounter with her father. The father wakes and erupts, saying to the daughter, "Where the hell have you been?"

"Don't you remember?" she says. "You said that I could go to the birthday party as long as I was back by 11 p.m., and it's 11 p.m. now." The father, outraged at hearing what the daughter has said, proceeds to chase the daughter, swinging his fists wildly at her. After an ugly altercation, the daughter manages to lock herself in her room and begins to cry, while her father, once again, passes out on the couch.

Several minutes later there is a knock at the daughter's door. "It's me, honey," says her visiting aunt. "Let me in." The daughter opens the door and falls into the arms of the aunt, crying hysterically. Finally the daughter composes herself and says, "If only I could find a way to not make him mad, he would love me."

"If only I could find a way…he would love me." It is not our job to find a way to make our partners feel better about themselves. Only they can do that. At best, we can provide them with a secure, loving relationship in which they can feel safe to express themselves to us. This, however, needs to be a relationship that is not judgmental or highly critical, and one in which our partner feels, on an ongoing basis, that we have their best interest at heart.

The Mindful Way: Emotionally Dependent Relationships

All of you are perfect just as you are, and you could use a little improvement.

Shunryu Suzuki Roshi

- Close your eyes. Begin mindful breathing. Be aware of breathing in and breathing out—just rest your awareness there.
- Now let your awareness shift to the relationships in your life.
- *Recognize* the major relationships you maintain in your life.
- *Accept* these relationships without judgment.
- *Investigate* the nature of these relationships. Are you dependent on any of them for your emotional well-being? Are they a primary resource for your self-worth?
- *Non-identify* with these relationships. Know that they don't define you. Embrace your inner beauty.
- Let yourself simply feel the experience. And when you are ready, simply open your eyes.

Chapter Fourteen

Summer Camp:
The Family System

It was not uncommon for children growing up in New York City to spend the summer at a sleep-away camp, in either upstate New York or one of the surrounding states. Even though my family had very little money, my parents found a subsidized sleep-away camp in upstate New York and I started my camp experience at the age of eight. From downtown New York, the kids would board the bus and drive off to spend eight weeks in camp, leaving our parents waving goodbye. Each year, these were the best eight weeks of my life.

The first camp that I attended had a profound effect on my life and, I believe, contributed greatly to who I was to become. I like to refer to this camp as a "freedom camp," because that was what it was all about. Low-income kids, black and white, from all over the city attended this camp. The mere fact that it was an integrated camp was astonishing at that time. This camp had a "soul" like no other environment I had the privilege to inhabit. There were no tennis courts. There were no swimming pools. There was no archery or many of the other typical amenities that made summer camp so enjoyable. There was a lake, a ball field (which was mostly dirt and crab-grass), a mess hall, and a rec hall. We lived in bunks, eight to ten same-gender kids to a bunk, which had cots with army blankets. The bathrooms and showers were usually located within a few hundred yards of a bunk.

Each morning we would roll out of bed at around 7:00 a.m. and walk down to the flag-pole. We would gather around the flag-pole and, while raising the flag, would sing folk songs or gospel songs. We would then make our way to the mess hall to eat breakfast. After breakfast, it was back to the bunk to make our beds and clean the bunk. Then the most remarkable thing would occur. Our counselor, an African from Kenya who taught me how to speak Swahili ("Jambo" is all I can remember) and could climb branchless trees with his bare feet, would ask us what we wanted to do that day. Imagine asking ten eight- and nine-year-olds what they wanted to do that day and going through a process that led to consensus. But each day that's what we did.

There was some structure. Meals were always at the same time. Every afternoon we had swim time in the lake, and every evening after dinner we had "free time" for an hour, in which we could do anything we liked. The day would usually close with an activity in the rec hall, concluding with a rousing rendition of "We Shall Overcome." On very special occasions we would close the evening with Pete Seeger's song, "Last Night I Had the Strangest Dream."

On Hiroshima Day (I didn't even know that there was a Hiroshima Day), we all wore black arm bands. Pete Seeger, the legendary folk singer, songwriter, and political activist, would visit the camp and give a free concert. One year, he even recorded a concert from the camp's rec hall.

What an amazing experience for a kid from a lower-middle-class neighborhood in New York City to have. It truly expanded my worldview. Just as important as expanding my worldview, it allowed me to be somebody other than who I was at home. For eight weeks every year, I was a different person. No longer did I have the influence of my family inducing me to be a certain way. No longer did my neighborhood dictate who I had to be. I was free to be me. Each year upon my return to NYC, I vowed to continue to be me. And each year, as does the fading of a tan, I would gradually fade back to who I was within my family and community system.

No one seemed to do anything conspicuously to bring me back, but back I came. Gone was the independent, self-confident boy I was at camp. I had loving parents, but the orbit of the family system quickly brought me back into alignment. Remember the teenage client I discussed earlier and how his family system created obstacles to prevent him from changing? He came to me looking like a Satan worshiper, and as he improved, his family system tried to pull him back into his appointed family role. This process is rarely conscious, but it happens nonetheless.

We live in systems: countries, states or regions, townships and communities, and family. All have an impact on who we are and who we become. All abide by certain constructs: some universal, others specific to the culture. The power of these systems is vast, and often we are unaware of the effect they are having, or have had, on who we are or how we think or feel.

The Family System

What's in a system? When I looked up the definition of the word "system," there were many. One definition is "the prevailing structure of society." So I researched the term "social structure" and found an interesting sociological quandary.

Within the field of sociology, there is a fundamental debate that centers around the concept of "structure" and a concept known as "agency," and the impact either has on human behavior and thought. In this context, structure seems to be based on constructs that help define our thinking, behavior, and attitudes, such as religion, social class, cultural norms, customs, gender expectations, etc. These constructs shape who we are by essentially influencing or limiting our beliefs and choices. Agency, on the other hand, refers to the capacity of individuals to act independently and to make their own free choices. The debate centers on which of these two concepts, structure versus agency, has more impact on human development and human behavior.

Murray Bowen, a psychiatrist and a professor, developed a theory of family systems that in many ways is based on the very debate of structure versus agency. Bowen was particularly interested in a concept he referred to as "differentiation." Differentiation refers to a person's ability to manage their own thoughts and emotions within the context of the family system. The more a person is capable of doing this, the more differentiated (autonomous) they are. The less they are able to do this, the more "fused" they are with the family system and the less able they are to fully manage their thoughts and feelings.

Life's journey is to become a whole human being. Humanistic psychologists refer to this as becoming self-actualized, realizing our full potential. The more differentiated and the more autonomous we become, the less emotionally dependent and therefore less anxious we are. This allows us to be better able to move towards meeting our true potential as a human being. From the moment of birth we are guided through this journey. Our journey begins with our family of origin. Some of us have better guides than others. Often, through no fault of their own, our guides are lacking in the awareness necessary to be a successful guide. Simply look at who guided them through their journey. Bowen actually addressed this issue. He called it the "multigenerational transmission process." This is a fancy term that means that the emotional landscape of a family system gets passed down (transmitted) from one generation to the next. If our parents' parents lacked the awareness necessary to support healthy emotional development, then it is likely that our parents lacked that awareness as well.

However, this pattern can be modified. We can become more aware. We can positively impact our children's journey or, for that matter, impact the journey of others in our lives. Parenthood is a nearly impossible task. Our ultimate challenge in parenting is to love our children as fully as we can, while at every moment preparing them to leave us. Ironically, it is similar to the challenge we face receiving the gift of life. Our ultimate challenge in life is living it to its fullest, despite knowing it can end at any moment. Perhaps the true challenge in parenting is to know how to blend structure, a set of principles to live by, and agency, the freedom to be oneself. How do we successfully create a container that is appropriately restrictive while at the same time supports individual freedom?

Containment

"What a little ball of energy." That's a familiar phrase. It's usually used to describe a youngster. When we are young, we are thought of as having unlimited energy. We bounce from one thing to the next with reckless abandon. And therein lies the problem: "reckless abandon." We don't want our young to be reckless. We don't want them to get hurt. So it is our responsibility to contain them. How we go about containing them is a major factor that can significantly influence their emotional well-being.

When I was in graduate school, I found it interesting to learn what type of family environment would be most likely to influence the development of an antisocial person (our criminal types). Certainly I assumed that if physical abuse existed in the family system, there would be a greater likelihood that a child might develop antisocial tendencies, and in fact, there is evidence to support this correlation. However, I also assumed that the family system would have an over controlling and dominant father. I had always been a strong advocate for adolescent rights and adolescent freedom and blanched at the thought that many parents, particularly fathers, were dictatorial in their behavior and attitude towards their children. So it came as a surprise to me to learn that the most likely family environment to influence antisocial behavior was characterized by "absence": absence of love, absence of caring, and absence of presence (particularly an absent father). Absence coupled with intermittent abuse is a real recipe for disaster.

When a child doesn't feel cared about, the development of their self-esteem can be significantly affected, and their feeling of hostility towards the world can increase. Pair this feeling with inappropriate supervision, and we may unleash the type of energy that materializes in the world as resentment, entitlement, and aggression—a bad combination.

Our children need to be supervised. Their behavior needs to be contained. Our obligation and responsibility to our children is to provide them with love, support, and guidance. But we must provide appropriate guidance, which is a balance between allowing and encouraging their expression of energy while containing and redirecting energy at the same time.

I recently saw a film called *How to Train Your Dragon*. This is an animated film that takes place in the days of the Vikings. It is the story of a Viking village and its continuous age-old battle with the dragons for survival. Their entire culture is based on dragon fighting. Of course, as it is with most dragon-fighting cultures, the best dragon fighters are held in the highest esteem by the villagers. As fate would have it, the chief of the village, a bold, powerful dragon fighter himself, has a son who doesn't quite fit the image of a dragon fighter. The son, a young adolescent, is much more intellectual and heartfelt. To limit any harm to his son and to reduce the amount of exposure the village has to the son, the father has made his son an apprentice, an indoor job requiring no dragon-fighting skills. However, the son desperately wants to fit in, wants his father's approval, and wants to fight dragons. After a confrontation with his father, in which his father chastises his son for resisting his demands that he stay clear of the battlefield, the boy is feeling exasperated. Under his breath he says, "You cannot contain the Viking energy without there being consequences."

So, how do we go about containing our own energy and the energy of our children in a way that maximizes the potential for emotional well-being? In the field of psychology, we call our ability to contain our behavior and reactivity "self-regulation" or, as discussed earlier, "emotional regulation." We maintain that an emotionally healthy person has the ability to self-regulate their behaviors, emotions, and desires, and functions in the world from a stable place. Freud coined the term "sublimation," which he described as the ability to transform libido (sexual energy) into socially acceptable behavior. In essence, Freudian theory suggests that we have to convert our innate, powerful sexual energy into socially acceptable acts, or we cannot survive as a civilized culture.

I believe that the concept of sublimation is fundamentally constructive, except for the fact that it focuses on the transformation of sexual energy instead of simply energy. We are all born with a reservoir of energy that we are naturally oriented to express. Observe an infant. Unless they are sleeping, they are rarely still. They are continually expressing their energy. And energy begets energy. When we express our energy in a non-destructive manner, we create energy. When we participate in activities that we truly enjoy, we get energy from our participation. However, so much of our life appears to be constructed in a manner that controls our expression of energy. To be a civilized society we have created "order," order based on rules and regulations and social appropriateness.

We seem to begin learning these rules from the moment of our birth. Think about all of the constructs that have been developed regarding proper mothering. For example, let's examine the construct of "scheduled feedings." For most of the twentieth century the prevailing attitude of our experts was that babies should be fed on a strict schedule. The "rule" was only feed the baby according to a schedule and not on demand. These days most experts support the opposite position, the demand schedule (when the baby is hungry, the baby will let you know and that is when the baby needs to be fed).

I remember reading an article in graduate school about a leading pediatrician in Germany in the 1950s who strongly advocated for the use of a "sleep board" for children. Each night the child would be strapped onto this board so the child's back would be kept straight, ensuring proper posture. How's that for an example of containing energy?

There is a cost to all this. Without an appropriate balance between an environment that supports the free-flowing expression of our energy, and the loving, supportive guidance, that gently influences our energy in the right direction, there will be consequences (as so eloquently stated by our adolescent Viking boy).

Back to Summer Camp

When I was fifteen years old, my best friend at summer camp and I had an opportunity to become CITs (counselors in training) at one of those "fancy" summer camps. This camp was located in the beautiful countryside of Western Massachusetts and had it all. It was built on a beautiful lake, offered water skiing and horseback riding, and had multiple baseball fields as well as other sport-related facilities and cabins with bathrooms. It was a chance to see how the other side lived, and best of all, because we would be CITs, it was free. So we decided that after seven years at our beloved freedom camp, it was time to venture out into the world for a different kind of experience.

We were assigned to a cabin and worked under the supervision of two counselors. One of these counselors was the hippest guy in camp. He was the "cool" guy that all the female counselors, and probably campers as well, swooned over. He drove a red Mustang, had rippling muscles, and walked with a swagger. Everybody wanted to be liked by him, and I was no exception. For reasons unknown (at the time), it was not that easy for me to relate to him. It took a while for the both of us to warm to each other. But eventually we did.

Each year this summer camp would conclude with a grand event called "Color War." I had never heard of Color War, and certainly my freedom camp would never have an event with the word "war" in the title. Color War was a weeklong event in which the entire camp was divided into two teams, each represented by a color. The two teams spent the week competing for points against one another in every way imaginable. Of course, these competitions included the standard events by age groups, such as swim meets, baseball, tennis, and all other types of sporting events. But the competition also included some very creative events such as the "Apache Relay" (not very politically correct by today's standards) and "Sing."

The Apache Relay was an all-day event in which each team had to complete a relay race of sorts that included dozens of unusual activities. These activities would include things like "duck waddle," which would require you to waddle down to the lake, in a crouched position, hands behind your legs, with a spoon in your mouth carrying an egg. If you dropped and broke the egg, you would have to start all over again. Once down to the lake, you would pass the baton to a kid standing with a fishing pole, and it would be his task to catch a fish (that was my job). The Apache Relay would often conclude with the cutting in half of a huge log. This event was worth a substantial amount of points.

Color War concluded with the most inspirational event, "Sing." Usually two teams were close enough in points that Sing would determine the winner. Although Sing took place on the last night, the teams had been preparing for this event from the start. Sing required that each team write and perform several songs based on several themes. A panel of judges, comprised of the camp's administrators, would judge each song for creativity, quality of writing, and quality of performance. It was an amazing experience to witness what a group of kids could create and perform in a week's time. I loved Sing.

Color War, that summer, was indeed a great experience for me, but not without some significant emotional experiences. The week began in an inauspicious manner; my friend and I were left off the teams. Apparently, because we were CITs, not really campers and not really counselors, they didn't know what to do with us. And our "favorite" counselor forgot to bring our status to the attention of the "assigning committee" who determines who is on each team. My friend and I were quite dismayed. All summer long we had heard, and spoken about, this grand event known as Color War. We felt overlooked and left out. And when we voiced our feelings to our counselor, his response was "So, what's the big deal?" There's empathy for you.

A senior boys' softball game was coming up on the Color War schedule. Most of these boys were about our age, and it seemed a good opportunity to appeal to the committee to assign each of us to one of the teams and allow us to play in this game. We convinced our counselor to speak to the assigning committee and advocate for us to be included in this event. He told the committee, "One of these CITs is a very good pitcher, and one is a very good first baseman." As it turned out, one team needed a pitcher and the other needed a first baseman. So it was decided by the committee to assign us to different teams and allow us to participate in the rest of the Color War events.

That was a glorious day for me, save one comment made to me by my counselor. I played first base, and, if I do say so, I played first base very well. One of the tasks of a good first baseman is to keep your infield players alert and relaxed. You do this through a process known as "chatter." Chatter is just that. It's a steady stream of low volume talking designed to inform and relax your players. It's not "trash talk," which is designed to insult or intimidate your opponent with the intent of negatively influencing his performance. It's chatter, good old American baseball talk. Despite batting in the sixth slot, which was difficult for me because I was "attached" to being a clean-up hitter (batting fourth) and a bit insulted that I was dropped down to sixth, I went four-for-four that day, with six runs batted in and a grand-slam homerun. I was in my element. I was in a zone. Midway through the game, after having hit my grand-slam homerun, I was playing the field at first base. As I had done all game, I was participating in chatter, "Hey, batter, batter; hey, batter, batter. Come on, strike him out." From the corner of my eye, I noticed a familiar motion, the swagger of my counselor. He hadn't been around much during the game and certainly hadn't displayed much interest in how the game was progressing. In fact, although he was approaching me, it was a result of his decision to leave the field and go elsewhere. I happened to be in his path. As he walked by me, he stopped momentarily and said the following words, words that echo to this day though many decades have passed: "Hey, contain yourself. I had to make a good argument to get you guys to play. Cool it." And with those words, he vanished. It was as if someone had stuck me with a pin and let my wind out.

That day, I was really having a good time. I wasn't hurting anybody. I wasn't offending anybody. Suddenly, without apparent justification, the parental figure, the authority figure, tells me to rein it in. Now, several decades later, I still remember that encounter. So what was so significant about it? Why did it affect me then, and why am I still talking about it? Obviously my reaction had to result from my counselor's insistence that I contain myself. And obviously, I had to have developed a degree of sensitivity associated with someone wanting to contain me. And of course, that someone had to be in my family of origin. Here we are again, back to the family system.

If our true nature is to express ourselves, to express our energy into the universe, then what can influence our ability to do so? And what are the likely consequences to us once our ability to express our energy is negatively influenced?

Containing Nature

What does nature teach us about this issue? As a result of living in California, I have become very familiar with the devastation that wildfires can cause. Virtually every year there is a major wildfire that wrecks havoc on the environment and the towns that inhabit the area. When a major fire breaks out, the news provides substantial coverage about the fire and the efforts to "contain" the fire. As a way for the viewers to have an understanding of the progress being made to fight the fire, news reporters will actually report the percentage to which the fire is contained. The higher the percentage, the more the fire is contained and therefore controlled. When a fire is raging, our desire is to get it under control. Interestingly, the official policy regarding wildfires has changed. Historically the policy was to fight the fire, contain and control it, until it could be extinguished. Now the official policy is, unless the fire is a threat to human inhabitants, watch it and let it burn. The philosophy is that the fire is actually good for the forest and should not be contained. The energy of a wildfire helps to regenerate the forest and is part of the natural order of the universe.

We need to be cognizant of the language we use. We "fight," "contain," "control," and "extinguish" a fire. When we describe the process of taming a horse, we say that we "break" a horse. When we break a horse, our desire is to gain total control over the behavior of the horse without breaking the spirit of the animal. Once again, there exists a delicate balance between discipline and preserving spirit and energy (structure versus agency).

Are these processes so much different than what takes place in the average family system? As parents, we have a responsibility to supervise, control, and contain our children. The number of times in a single day that we admonish certain behaviors is countless. Often times the admonishment is nonverbal, a certain look or energy. Even when we do this with love and understanding (as we always hope to do), the end result is containment.

As we discussed earlier, appropriate containment demonstrates that the child is cared for. But what if there is too little or no containment, or too much containment? If there is no containment, the unsupervised, undisciplined, uncared-for child can develop very dysfunctional behavior. If the containment is too much, or if the containment is delivered through aggression, criticism, hostility, "put downs," or a rigid authoritarian attitude, emotional problems can develop as well. It may surprise you to learn that until the eminent American pediatrician Dr. Benjamin Spock wrote a bestselling parenting book in 1946, which extolled the virtues of treating children with respect and as individuals and providing them with affection, the prevailing child-rearing attitude was purely disciplinarian. Much of what Spock advocated was the building of the child's self-esteem. This was a far cry from the prevailing attitude "children should be seen and not heard."

Excessive containment can have consequences, including an increase in anxiety and hostility and learned helplessness. Think of a child or adolescent who reacts to a situation by putting their hand through the wall, a violent burst of energy caused by extreme frustration. When I was a child, every time I saw a new wall hanging in my house, I knew that my mother was covering a hole punched in the wall by my brother. We had quite a few wall hangings.

The art of containing is a complicated process. Early in our lifecycle, containment is a simple act of ongoing control. Once our infants are mobile, we tend to watch them like a hawk, monitoring their behavior, so they won't get hurt or destroy something in their path. There is not a lot of need for explanation. We tend to simply say "no" and move them in a direction that is most comfortable for our own emotional well-being. But as they age, this process gets more complicated. They start asking "why," and some can be very sensitive to the injustice of control. Often we just say "because I said so," and offer no explanation at all. Too much of this approach can leave a child feeling powerless and angry.

I have had many clients whose anxiety seems to have been influenced by this type of parenting approach. To make matters worse, often these parents were inconsistent, one moment permissive and easygoing, and the next rigid and controlling. We all have a river of energy within us that needs to be expressed and released. When a river is dammed up and its source keeps flowing, this can lead to a bad situation: the bursting of the dam. Feeling contained can lead to intense feelings of anger. I believe that many of us act impulsively because we just want to express our energy and we are tired of containing ourselves. However, if we create a life in which we can express our energy through relationships, career, community, and adventure, and through naturally grounding activities such as meditation, yoga, or long walks through the woods, we are less likely to burst.

The Dog and the Invisible Fence

A friend of mine lives in a lovely wooded area. His house sits atop a ridge overlooking his property. His property is dotted with pine trees, and his driveway cuts through the middle of his property. My friend owns a large dog, who needs to roam. However, the configuration of the property made it very difficult to build a fence. His solution was to set up an invisible electric fence.

The electric fence system operates by creating a perimeter of electrical current around the property. The dog wears a collar that is outfitted with a device that picks up the current and, as a result, delivers a shock. Most dogs learn not to approach the fence after only a few trial and errors. The fence seems to work very well and the dog is appropriately contained. One day, when I was visiting my friend, I witnessed an occurrence that left me pondering containment. On a beautiful summer's day, my friend and I were sitting on his deck. His dog was romping around the property. The electric fence was activated and the dog was wearing his collar. Suddenly, just outside the boundary of the fence, a jackrabbit ran across the woods. The dog lurched after it, stopping only inches from the electric fence. He then paced frantically back and forth, whining and crying, desperately wanting to give chase to the jackrabbit. My friend called out, admonishing the dog and beseeching him to quiet down and behave. Eventually, the dog settled down and his whimpering faded to an occasional sigh.

What I had just witnessed seemed to be a dilemma that many of us face from time to time. Most parents face this dilemma with their toddlers every day. From the dog's perspective, his reaction was natural. He was expressing his dog nature. Dogs chase rabbits. But he was unable to fulfill his dog nature, and as a result he experienced frustration and anxiety.

From my friend's perspective, he can't have a dog that runs wild and kills rabbits: hence the fence. His admonishment of the dog served as a reinforcement that he was in charge and that the dog needed to behave.

The good news is that my friend dearly loves his dog. He takes him on long walks and gives him nutritious dog food and plenty of treats, accompanied by hugs and kisses. The balance between containing his dog's dog nature and providing his dog love and affection seems to be working.

On a side note, I have a large dog that has been raised with a rabbit. They are often in very close proximity and seem to have a real fondness for each other. My dog doesn't chase rabbits. Perhaps this scenario can give us a little insight regarding how we can change that which we think is our nature.

The Mindful Way: Containment

- Close your eyes. Begin mindful breathing. Be aware of breathing in and breathing out—just rest your awareness there.
- Now shift your awareness and think about an area of your life in which you feel particularly contained. What are the emotions surrounding this containment? Where do you feel it in your body? What color is it?
- Just sit with this experience.
- Investigate this containment. Are there benefits and/or consequences as a result of this containment? Can you modify this situation and "free up" your energy without causing harm to yourself or others? What actions can you take to accomplish this?
- Now shift your awareness to other areas of your life. Do you feel overly contained in these areas as well, or is there balance in your life? What could you do to bring balance into your life?
- Sit with this as long as you need. When you are ready, open your eyes.
- Write down the areas of your life in which you feel particularly contained and what you can do to free up your energy in these areas.

A Bag of Nails: Anger

Once upon a time, there was a little boy with a bad temper. The boy's father wanted to teach him a lesson, so he gave him a bag of nails and told him that every time he lost his temper, he must hammer a nail into the fence. The first day, the boy had driven thirty-seven nails into the fence. He was really mad. Gradually, the little boy discovered it was easier to hold his temper than to drive those nails into the fence, and the number of daily nails dwindled down.

The day finally came when the little boy didn't lose his temper even once. He became so proud of himself, and he couldn't wait to tell his father. His father was pleased, but suggested that he now pull out one nail for each day that he could hold his temper. The days passed, and the young boy was finally able to tell his father that all the nails were gone. The father took his son by the hand and led him to the fence.

"You have done well, my son," he said, "but look at the holes in the fence. The fence will never be the same." The little boy listened carefully as his father continued to speak. "When you say things in anger, they leave a scar just like these. You can put a knife in a man and draw it out, but no matter how many times you say, 'I'm sorry,' the wound will still be there."[31]

Anger and Emotional Well-Being

As so eloquently displayed in the Bag of Nails story, anger can be a negative and destructive force. Research has shown that anger is correlated to increases in heart disease, stroke, and other potentially deadly diseases, and can compromise the immune system. It is an emotion that is often misunderstood and, since it is a primary emotion, has been touted by some as being "healthy" and others as not.

When I was attending graduate school, the prevailing attitude was that the expression of anger was a healthy process. I was taught numerous techniques to help a client get "in touch" with their anger and then express it. It would not be an uncommon practice to hand a client a plastic bat and an overstuffed pillow, suggest that the client imagine that the pillow represented someone or something, and instruct the client to strike the pillow as hard and as often as they could to release their pent-up anger. Fortunately, despite my training, it did not take many of these types of sessions for me to intuitively know that this process was not helpful and, in fact, could be emotionally damaging.

The culmination of this realization came when I encountered a client who had a very abusive, humiliating past. He was a middle-aged man, small in stature but quite muscular, who presented himself in a very controlled and contained manner. He appeared "cut off" from his feelings, the perfect candidate to use a technique to help him express his anger. But something intuitively told me not to go there. I knew that exciting this man and having him express his anger would not be beneficial to him. Instead I decided to discuss my observations, specifically my observation that he appeared to be somewhat cut off from his feelings and somewhat tense and "pent up." He received this information without any negative reaction and, in fact, supported my observations, stating, "Welcome to my world."

I asked him what, if anything, he had done to address these issues. He informed me that many years ago he had been in therapy. In fact, he had gone through a fairly well-known, intensive ten-week psychotherapy group process that I was fairly knowledgeable about. He focused on the ten-week intensive psychotherapy group process and told me the following story.

> The group-process program was very structured. We would meet each week for three hours in an old warehouse in downtown San Francisco. We met in the evening, in a large open room on the fifth floor, when the building was less occupied by other tenants. This allowed us to yell and scream without upsetting anyone. They called it 'primal therapy.' I didn't know much about it, except that you were supposed to yell as loud as you could when the time was right.
>
> There was a workbook we took home each week, and we had to do assignments in the book. Every week someone was picked to work on their stuff. Mostly we would work on family of origin stuff: you know, how your mother and father screwed you up and how important it was that you told them how you felt about it.
>
> Each week we would do what was called "psychodrama," where a member of the group would play a member of your family of origin, and you could interact with them and tell them how you felt about them. The whole thing made me uncomfortable. But they kept saying that that was natural and even good, even though I didn't think so. So, after about five weeks, I guess it was my turn to work. I told them again that it made me uncomfortable, but they said that I shouldn't worry about it and they would help me work through it.

We set up a scene from my childhood with group members playing my father, mother, and brothers and sisters. I can't really remember what the whole scene was about. But what I do remember is that towards the end of this encounter the group leader came into the middle of the psychodrama, handed me a bat, and pointed to a big pillow and said, "I want you to imagine that that pillow is your mother. Now I want you to kill your mother!"

I was stunned. He kept saying, "Don't worry about it; you can do this. It will be good for you." He kept pushing me until I took the bat and beat that pillow to shreds. "Well done," I finally heard him say, as I literally stood shaking in my boots.

The session ended and everybody left. I was the last to leave. I took a moment to try and compose myself. I walked out into the hall, pressed the elevator button, and waited for it to come. I heard a beep as the elevator doors opened. I walked into the elevator and stood just inside the doors as they closed. The elevator went down two floors and stopped. The doors opened, and this rather tall guy walked into the elevator, brushing my shoulder as he went by. I saw red. Without me even knowing, I grabbed this guy by the throat and lifted him off the floor. He dangled against the elevator wall, his face turning beet red. Finally, the elevator landed on the first floor. The doors opened and I realized what I was doing. I let go of the guy and he backed away from me, apparently okay. I turned and left the elevator. I never went back to that group.

Obviously, hearing this story was horrifying. I felt compassion for my client and his elevator victim, and upset at the group leaders for being so self-righteously invested in their therapy process (which, by the way, had been stopped). This was a classic example of anger begetting anger.

What my client needed to learn were methods that could help calm and ground him, not how to incite his anger. He needed a much gentler approach, one that allowed him to feel safe and begin to relax his defensive posture towards the world. As we become more relaxed and our body becomes less tense, we are able to open our heart and share our energy with the world, as well as let in energy that can be restorative. Remember the shields on the starship Enterprise? Nothing could get in, but nothing could get out either, and the energy it took to maintain the shields was extremely taxing.

I worked with this client for many months, focusing simply on allowing him to feel safe with me and safe with himself. We would open each session with a relaxation process that focused on his breathing. I helped him to imagine and design a safe place within, a place he could enter and feel totally safe. Over time, in a place of calm, he began to discuss the horrors of his childhood. We went very slowly, and each time he appeared to get agitated, we simply went back to a calm place.

Eventually he was able to talk about distressing events without becoming distressed. His demeanor began to change. He was no longer the tense, reactive, guarded individual who first walked into my office. As a result, he was no longer quick to react in anger. He was able to develop an awareness regarding his anger and to become mindful of his reactivity. When he felt angry, he paused for a moment and would say to himself, "I feel angry; what's going on?" This simple interruption, this pause, allowed him to choose to do something other than to get angry.

Many things can make us feel angry. Our anger can even be activated when we find ourselves exposed to anger. And the anger doesn't have to be directed towards us. An atmosphere of anger and aggression will often produce anger and aggression in those who have been exposed to it.

Much research has been conducted to determine the effects of simply witnessing or being exposed to excessive violence or anger. Published findings demonstrate that violent crime rises sharply during the twelve hours following a heavyweight championship fight.

A Life Crisis

Years ago I was faced with a crisis in my life. My father, age sixty-three, had suffered a massive heart attack and was not expected to survive. When I reached the hospital, I was met by my father's doctor who told me, in a very calm and compassionate manner, that my father's condition was grave. He said that each day my father lived would give him a 10-percent chance of surviving, and that if he lived for ten days, he would recover. This doctor was from India. He possessed a very calm demeanor. When relating to him, I felt his full attention. His energy was radiant. Each day upon my arrival at the hospital, I was met by this doctor with a nod and a smile. My father survived those ten days and was released from the hospital.

After returning home, my father was reassigned to a new doctor because of his insurance plan. I accompanied my father to his first visit with the doctor. The doctor was a highly trained heart specialist. He was obviously very bright and well educated. He was very energetic, intense, and moved and communicated at a rapid pace. He was very familiar with my father's chart and condition and began to lay out his approach to the situation.

He explained to my father that he wanted to take a very "aggressive" approach in "fighting" my father's heart disease. He wanted my father to start a regimen of exercise that would include aerobics and weight training and to radically change his diet. "This indeed will be a significant lifestyle change," he said.

My father and I listened to the doctor's plan. After we left the appointment, my father asked for my opinion about what we just heard. I could see that he was feeling a little uncomfortable. I asked him about his concerns. He told me that although this new doctor seemed very confident, his approach was radically different from his former doctor's. I suggested that we make an appointment with his first doctor to discuss these differences, which we did.

We arrived at the appointment with my father's first doctor and were greeted with a lovely smile and a nod. "Please do come in," he said. We sat for a while, simply chatting about things and how my father was doing. Eventually my father discussed what he had come to discuss: the radically different approach his new doctor wanted to take. Sensitive to the situation, the doctor said, "I am sure that you are in very competent hands; however, if you are asking me how I would approach your care, I can summarize that in a few words: *take it easy.*" He went on to say, "Slow everything down. You have just survived a major trauma. Relax; go for short gentle walks. Eat less and, of course, eat right. Adopt an attitude that is more carefree and less stressed, and this will serve you well."

We thanked the doctor and left his office. Upon our return home, my father called his insurance carrier and insisted that he be allowed to continue under the care of his first doctor. They agreed. My father opted to take the "calm" approach to deal with his heart condition. He lived ten quality years before he finally succumbed to heart failure, and I believe those years were a result of following his doctor's advice to "live calm."

Reactivity and Anger

Anger is reactive. It is the opposite of calm. It often takes flight without us even realizing it. Many of us relish our anger. It feels good to express our anger because we are tired of always constricting our emotions (containment). We simply want to be free to express how we feel without worrying about the consequences. But there are consequences, and they can be significant. Not only can expressed anger damage the person to whom it is directed, but it can be damaging to the person expressing it. It often leaves us feeling bad about ourselves and therefore not good for our self-esteem.

We need to find ways to stem the flow of anger and interrupt it before it takes hold and is launched into the environment. There are several ways to accomplish this. For example, techniques that interrupt our reactivity, such as counting to ten before we react, or taking a walk around the block, or sitting and breathing to calm ourselves, are often effective ways to stop an angry response.

Awareness is another way to stop an angry response. Being mindful of our anger and attuning to our feelings is an effective way to lessen our anger. If we are able to recognize that we are becoming angry, we can take measures to stop its emergence. We can create an internal dialog designed to mitigate the angry feelings. We may say to ourselves, "Take it easy," or "It's no big deal," or we may cast the offending individual in a different light that helps dissipate our anger, i.e., "He's doing the best he can." I once instructed an adult client, who often became enraged by his mother's antics, to think, "You poor, pathetic individual; life must be very hard for you." He no longer reacted with anger towards his mother.

For many years, I have counseled my clients that "*beneath all anger is hurt.*" Uncovering what has been hurtful and expressing this sentiment rather than anger creates a dynamic that has a greater chance of being heard and actually being experienced by the person to whom you are expressing your feelings. People are more receptive to hearing about our feelings of hurt than they are receptive to our anger. We have all been hurt, and therefore we can all relate to hurt. And if we are able to express this hurt without blaming the other person by simply making an "I" statement (I feel hurt) rather than a "you" statement (you hurt me), we can maximize the effectiveness of expressing our feelings.

When we are angry, we are tense. Chronic anger is often a result of feeling frustrated with life's circumstances. This leaves us with very little tolerance for life's challenges. Living with a constant flow of angry feelings can affect our daily routines, such as our sleeping habits, and in turn can affect our level of anger. For example, show me a parent who is sleep deprived and overwhelmed by parenting responsibilities, and I'll show you a person who is much more likely to react with anger. Show me a parent who is calm, rested, and has the support needed to accomplish the task of parenting, and I'll show you a person who is much less likely to react in anger.

We need to be compassionate with ourselves. We need to be aware of our environment and whether we are becoming tense. And if so, we need to intervene effectively to alleviate the tension or simply interrupt the buildup of tension.

Remember the flight attendant's instructions: "Put your own oxygen mask on first before attending to your child." Daily exercise, meditation, or hiking can provide hours of relief from tension buildup and ultimately reduce feelings of anger.

Power Struggles

After years of working in therapy with couples, I have learned to discern the difference between an argument and a power struggle. Certainly most couples in healthy relationships have arguments. However, I don't subscribe to the notion that constant arguing or the expression of anger on an ongoing basis is either healthy in and of itself or a sign of a healthy relationship. In my opinion, the belief that people need to get in touch with their anger and express their anger is overrated. It is an oversimplification of a complex process.

As previously stated, what resides beneath our feeling of anger is hurt. Identify the hurt and how we perceived events that led to feeling hurt, and we are likely to find the source of our angry feelings. When we are able to identify the hurt, we can express our pain rather than our anger. The expression of anger usually closes a door, the door to the emotional life of the person to whom we are expressing our anger. In order to resolve conflict, we want to keep that door open.

A power struggle is an extreme example of the expression of anger between two people. It rarely matters what the couple is even fighting about; the intensity of the anger is high. The essential problem isn't just the expressed anger. The essential problem is where the anger is directed, and how the anger is used to "attack" the other person's sense of self-worth. This type of encounter is not just about winning an argument. This type of encounter is about winning a fight at the expense of the other person's self-worth.

During a power struggle, each member of the couple is motivated to protect their own sense of worth, while attacking their partner's character. Resolution of the issue actually becomes secondary to wanting the *satisfaction* of winning the fight at the expense of the partner. To bolster their own self-worth, the winner needs to feel that he or she was right, while the loser not only needs to acknowledge that they were wrong, but that this wrongness is a reflection of a flaw in their makeup. This process is rarely conscious. The couple actually believes that they are fighting about an issue, and that's that.

As a couples therapist, I have witnessed numerous power struggles between couples. For example, I witnessed a high-intensity fight between a couple that had been going on for days. It began as a result of a disagreement as to whether the dinner steak was cooked "well done" or "medium." Each needed the other to admit that they were wrong about how the steak was cooked, and each, unconsciously, was communicating to the other that their incorrect view was a result of their faulty character and their deficiency as a person.

Obviously, power struggles within a couple system are a bad sign. They signal that the members of a couple are harboring deeply held resentments towards one another. They often signal issues of control between the couple, and that the balance of power between the couple is inequitable. This inequality in the relationship is personal. This means that one member feels "better than" the other member and, as a result, devalues their partner. And the other member senses that their partner feels this way. This places one member in a "more-than" position and the other member in a "less-than" position. So much for feeling that your partner has your best interest at heart and that you are in a relationship based on unconditional love.

Dr. John Gottman, Professor Emeritus of Psychology at the University of Washington and co-founder of The Gottman Institute, is world renowned for his work on marital stability and divorce prediction. He has conducted extensive research with couples to determine what qualities are likely predictors of divorce. He identified four most-likely predictors of a troubled marriage that he calls the "Four Horsemen": defensiveness, stonewalling, criticism, and contempt.

Of the four, Gottman has identified contempt as being the most predictive behavior of divorce. Gottman states, "You would think that criticism would be the worst, because criticism is a global condemnation of a person's character. Yet contempt is qualitatively different from criticism. With criticism I might say to my wife, 'You never listen; you are really selfish and insensitive.' Well, she's going to respond defensively to that. That's not very good for our problem solving and interaction. But if I speak from a superior plane, that's far more damaging, and contempt is any statement made from a higher level."

Ultimately, power struggles seem to result from a high level of emotional dependency between a couple and unmet expectations. These couples seem to have a nonverbal contract to make one another feel good about themselves and to bolster each other's self-esteem, just like George and Martha from the film *Who's Afraid of Virginia Woolf.* However, when this process of contributing to the worth of the partner breaks down, power struggles often begin.

Letting Go of Anger

People can change. People can become less angry. George Foreman, the Heavyweight Boxing Champion of the World, was a menacing figure. He was mean, angry, hostile, and aggressive. In 1974, George Foreman faced Muhammad Ali in a title fight that took place in Zaire, Africa, known as the "Rumble in the Jungle." Foreman, undefeated at the time with a record of forty wins and no losses, thirty-seven coming by way of knockout, was heavily favored to win the fight.

Ali endeared himself to the people of Zaire, making Foreman furious that he was not the center of attention. In an historic event, Ali defeated Foreman in the eighth round of the fight and reclaimed the Heavyweight Champion title. Foreman was devastated by his defeat. His invincibility had been shattered.

Although Foreman continued to fight, he was never the same again. After a particularly grueling fight which he lost, Foreman claims to have had a near-death experience. He reported feeling hopeless and filled with despair. He pleaded with God to save him and reports that he felt God asking him to change his ways and convert his life. Some would call this experience Foreman's "dark night of the soul." He became a born-again Christian and eventually an ordained minister.

Today, George Foreman is a beloved public figure. He is a highly successful businessman, continues to preach at his church, has established youth centers, and frequently appears on national talk shows. He is now a beacon of light. His radiant smile can't help but make his viewers smile as well.

Whether fate or something else changed George Foreman from an extremely angry, hostile man to a lovable, approachable person is not the point. The point is that George Foreman changed. He changed from an individual who hurt people to a person who helps people. He changed from a person who was aloof and cold and walked around with a monstrous chip on his shoulder to a warm, endearing person who seems to value every moment of life. George Foreman changed his attitude. George Foreman changed his perspective on life and, with these changes, has been rewarded with love and warmth. If he can do it, we all can do it.

There is a saying: "For every minute you are angry, you lose sixty seconds of happiness." Remember this the next time you are about to become angry.

Fear leads to anger, anger leads to hate; hate leads to suffering.
Master Yoda, *Star Wars Episode V: The Empire Strikes Back*

The Mindful Way: Anger

- Close your eyes. Begin mindful breathing. Be aware of breathing in and breathing out—just rest your awareness there.
- Now let your awareness shift to your feelings of anger.

- *Recognize* your anger.
- *Accept* your anger.
- *Investigate* your anger. What makes you angry?
- *Non-identify* with your anger. You are not an angry person. You are a person who is experiencing anger.
- Now let yourself go beneath the anger to the hurt or disappointment. Where do you experience this in your body? What kind of feeling is it in your body? What color is it? Just sit with it.
- Now name the hurt. I feel angry because I am hurt, and I am hurt about...
- Sit with your hurt. Accept the feeling. Be aware of any changes in your body as you accept the feeling. Is the hurt feeling dissipating or changing in any way?
- When you are ready, open your eyes.

You may want to write about your experience, concentrating on the hurt and pain caused by a situation rather than the resulting anger. Write about how you could express the hurt and not the anger.

The next time you feel anger, use the STOP method:

- **S**top and interrupt the automatic pilot by concentrating on the present moment.
- **T**ake a breath and bring attention on the experience of the "in-and-out" breath.
- **O**pen to observation. Connect to the experience of this moment and inquire with a sense of curiosity:
  - What am I seeing?
  - What am I feeling?
  - What am I sensing?

- o   What am I hearing?
- o   What am I smelling?
- o   What am I thinking?
- **P**roceed

Chapter Sixteen

'Tis Better to Give than Receive: Giving

Many years ago in a rural province of India, there was a monastery situated high in the mountains. It was a rather poor community, but each year it managed to survive. One day word arrived that the taxes on the land had been significantly raised, and the community would have only a certain amount of time to pay these taxes before the land would be taken from them. This caused terrible upset and no one knew what to do.

In a land thousands of miles from the monastery, a wealthy businessman, who recently began to develop a spiritual practice, heard of the problem facing the community. He had studied several of the writings of the master of the monastery and was drawn to his teachings. He decided to take a pilgrimage to India and pay all of the necessary taxes to save the monastery. He boarded a plane and flew to Bombay.

Bombay was several days' journey from the mountainous destination he sought. He hired a guide and provisioned a pack animal, and together they rode through the mountains to reach their goal. On the fourth day, after a grueling journey, they arrived. They were tired and dirty. They were greeted with open arms and given hot tea and nourishment. After a short while, the businessman asked about the location of the master. "He has gone to seek solitude and to meditate," said the master's disciple. "But I have wonderful news," said the businessman, "and must see him now." The disciple, not wanting to offend the businessman, directed him to the opening of a large cave. "The master sits in there," he said.

The businessman walked over to his steed and unhitched from the saddle two large cloth sacks filled with gold coins. Not knowing the currency of the province and, if truth be told, for dramatic effect, the businessman had decided to make his contribution in gold coins. With a sack in each hand, he proceeded to the cave. He reached the mouth of the cave and announced his presence. However, there was no response. He peered into the cave but could see very little, except that the cave appeared to be rather large and deep. He could see some light emanating from the back of the cave, so he decided to enter.

Feeling noble about his task, with sacks in hand, he proceeded. Due to the dim light, he made slow but steady progress. Finally he reached his destination, the rear of the cave. Sitting before him in a lotus position was the master. The businessman stood before the master, uncertain how to proceed. He was reticent to disturb the master's meditation, but he thought that the news and gift he brought were so wonderful that this disturbance would be immediately forgiven. He cleared his throat a few times and then said, "Master, master, I have wonderful news." The old sage opened his eyes, smiled, and said, "What have you come here to tell me?" The businessman held out his arms, the sacks filled with gold dangling from his hands.

"Master, I have brought gold. Enough gold for you to pay off all of the back taxes on this property and for future taxes as well," he said. The sage's expression was unchanged. The businessman placed each sack of gold on either side of the sage and waited. The master closed his eyes and resumed meditating.

The businessman did not know what to do. Finally he yelled out, "Master!" Opening his eyes once again, the sage replied, "Yes, can I help you?"

"Can you help me?" asked the businessman in a rather scornful voice. "I just gave you enough money to save your monastery and keep it afloat well into the future, and you ask, 'Can I help you?'"

"What is it you want from me?" asked the master.

"I want you to thank me," said the businessman.

"Thank you?" asked the sage. "Thank you for what?"

"Thank me for the generous gift I have bestowed upon you," said the businessman.

The master's face broke out into a huge smile, and with a gleam in his eyes, he said, "Oh, but it is you who should thank me for giving you the opportunity to give so generously." And with that statement the sage closed his eyes and resumed his meditation.

Giving

Throughout the years I have had several wealthy clients who have made significant contributions to specific charities. Many of these contributions were made anonymously. This is good and honorable behavior. Despite the fact that they had made me aware of their giving, they were not motivated by the need for recognition from me or the charity. They were actually motivated by a social construct that says that "a good person is a person who gives to charity" and the need to see themselves as a good person. People who give to charity are good people, just as people who don't are also good people, because after all, at our core we are all good people. However, needing to feel good about our actions, or needing to tell ourselves that we are good because we did a good thing, is still a form of external validation. In this scenario, fulfilling the social construct (do good things) acts as validation. It still represents a level of attachment that ultimately leaves us vulnerable to suffering. It is still ego driven.

From a practical standpoint, this is not a bad scenario. It is clearly more wholesome to be charitable than not, just as it is more wholesome to use exercise as a distraction from our emotional pain than to participate in self-destructive behaviors, such as abusing drugs or alcohol. However, wholesome giving is essentially mindless. Its origin does not come from our mind but from our true nature. It is not influenced by our social constructs. It is pure energy that emanates from our compassion, or our desire to, in some way, alleviate the suffering of others out of love and caring.

In the film *Ghost Writer*, there is a scene that is rather incidental to the plot of the story. The main character decides to go out and explore the island where he is temporarily staying. He is a guest of a very powerful, wealthy man. The scene revolves around an encounter between the main character and one of the servants of the household.

Standing in the garage, the main character asks the servant if he can borrow a bicycle to tour around the island. Concerned about the weather and the likelihood that a storm is coming, the servant suggests that he use the car and forego the bicycle. The servant's face shows a degree of surprise and concern when the main character insists on using the bike. Bewildered, the servant says, "Well, at least take my hat and gloves to keep yourself warm."

This simple little scene resonated with me. The servant's response and his motivation to give emanated from a place of compassion. With no thought to the welfare of his own property, he offered his hat and gloves from a place of concern and caring. For me, this represents what true giving is all about.

Giving and compassion can be an antidote to many of our negative emotions, including anger and depression. It may sound a bit clichéd, but it's not how much we give or what objects we give that is significant. What is significant is that we give. And what is ultimately essential to our emotional well-being is that we give of ourselves: our emotions, our compassion, our heartfelt energy.

The type of giving that can be emotionally healing is not based on a social construct that defines who we should be or how we should behave towards one another. It is not part of societal, cultural, or religious dogma. It is not motivated by living up to a standard that represents what a "good" person is. It is not even about expecting nothing in return. The healing property of giving is generated by our capacity to feel compassion and empathy toward another and to be moved from a heartfelt place to give. It is a flow of energy that comes from our "being," our true nature. As put so eloquently by author and poet Khalil Gibran, "You give but little when you give of your possessions. It is when you give of yourself that you truly give."[32]

Love and Giving

As we have previously discussed, often we operate from an emotional place of scarcity. We become very protective of our emotions and guarded against the possibility of getting emotionally hurt by another. We may anticipate that someone will take from us emotionally and give little in return. We may believe that we possess only a limited amount of love, and therefore we express our love very selectively. From this emotional stance, it is difficult to be heartfelt and open. This calls to mind the old adage, "Is it better to have loved and lost than never to have loved at all?" If you believe that we have an endless capacity to love, then the answer becomes obvious. But if you believe that our love is finite, and if we give it, it will be trampled on, we will choose not to have loved at all.

Love is a very powerful emotion. We all want it, even those that deny that they do. However, we seem to have gotten the importance of love backwards. By this I mean that we emphasize our need to be loved and deemphasize our need to feel love. Next time you are in a card shop, look at all the cards that say, "I love you." The intention is to assure the recipient that they are loved. Try to find a card that says, "Thank you for letting me feel love for you." The intention of this message is not to assure the recipient that they are loved, but to express how grateful the giver of the card is that they serve as an object of their love.

The difference between these two messages is significant. We are a culture that continually emphasizes the need to be loved. Some of us even struggle with the notion of whether we are worthy to be loved. But being loved, which is a powerful emotional feeling, pales by comparison to feeling love and perhaps having the opportunity to express our love. As the receiver, our experience is based on an external event, something emanating from outside of ourselves. By definition, this experience is one step removed. It is like making a recording of an original piece of music. The recording can never have as high a quality as the original piece. But when we feel love we have a direct internal experience. Our body fills with emotion, and we open up the floodgates and let ourselves bask in the experience. This is an amazing experience, one that triggers chemical responses in our body and one that allows us to feel alive and fully present. No wonder, as the song says, "We're addicted to love."

Don't confuse this process with the experience we have when love is mutual. Mutual love has two components, receiving love and giving love. We may respond to receiving love, or knowing that we are loved, by giving love in return. But it is still the same process. That is to say, it is the feeling generated by love, regardless of whether it is a response to receiving love, that makes the experience emotionally powerful.

Consider the following. A man is asked if he has ever been married, and he responds, "No." He is then asked if he has ever been in love, and he responds, "Yes." When asked to explain the circumstance of his love and why it never led to marriage, he says, "One evening when I was returning home from work on the train, I saw the most beautiful woman I have ever seen. Her skin was so fair, her eyes were as green as emeralds, and her hair was as golden as harvest wheat. I fell in love with her instantly, and I have never stopped loving her." "What was her name?" he is asked. His reply: "I don't know. I chose not to speak to her, yet I have loved her ever since."

Our need to feel love and to express our love seem to be essential elements of our true nature. However, at times our emotional makeup, or our insecurities, may orient us to seek love as a means to make us feel more secure and better about ourselves. "If I am loved, then I'm okay." Love in this manner is a powerful externally validating experience. This is another way in which we try to bolster our self-worth and feel more secure in a universe of impermanence.

This process is a remnant of our initial relationship: the relationship between mother and child. Unconsciously, we yearn to recreate this connection (mother/child), regardless of how we consciously evaluate that specific relationship. What this means is, even when we believe or recall that the relationship we had with our mother was unsatisfactory, we still strive on an unconscious level to recreate the "good" parts of that relationship.

An entire theoretical model of psychology entitled "object relations" is based primarily on this principle. This theory suggests that as infants we internalize representations of the objects (persons) with whom we are in relationship. These representations may or may not accurately represent reality, and they can also be compartmentalized. This means that the infant will develop an internal representation of the "good mother" as well as the "bad mother," and so on. What is salient to this discussion is that based on prior early childhood experience, which is not conscious, we are driven to develop relationships that recreate the feeling of being loved by the "good mother." This is why being loved is so important to us.

However, this process is a double-edged sword. On the one hand, a fundamental aspect to the development of self-esteem is the infant's experience of being comforted and supported, being loved, by the mother. High self-esteem is much more likely to develop when the infant receives from the mother consistent love and support, blended with an appropriate amount of support for the infant's individuation (the infant's need to develop as a separate human being). But this process is time sensitive. Its greatest impact occurs during the developmental stages of infancy and childhood. Once an adult, the process cannot be the same. Essentially, there's no going back.

What is being suggested here is that even when we are able to recreate a process that is similar to the original dynamics of relating to the "good mother," the impact on our self-esteem is not the same. To be clear, it is, of course, positive to be in relationship with someone who is supportive and loving. As stated earlier, these types of relationships are always good for us and can, to some degree, influence our feelings of self-worth, value, and esteem. But as an adult, relying on an outside source to provide us with a sense of security and to bolster our self-esteem is conditional. This reliance represents an external validation model, which means that we are dependent on the validating source. Remove the source, and all can quickly evaporate.

As an adult, the development of self-esteem, or the degree to which we love and value ourselves, must come from within. It is certainly helpful to be in an environment that will support this journey. However, the journey is ours and ours alone. To develop a greater sense of worth we need to give love to ourselves, continuously validating ourselves. It may take a long time for us to feel good about ourselves. Remember that the validating interaction between mother and infant occurs countless times over many years. Be patient and be loving.

Why We Love Our Pets So Much

If we need any evidence to substantiate the desire and need to give love, all we need do is look at our behavior towards our pets. Much of the Western world is "crazy" about their pets. Pet ownership has exploded, and entire industries have been developed to support this "love affair." But why are we so enamored by our pets? Is it because we want the added responsibilities that accompany pet ownership? Or is it because we want the added expense that pet ownership requires? We know that these can't be the motivation to own a pet. We know that the primary motivation to own a pet is love. And we love to love our pets.

I once had a client who was a very high-powered attorney. He wore expensive suits, maintained a very high profile, and only represented the most wealthy, influential clients. He was known as a fierce litigator, and his reputation served him so well that he almost always settled his cases before entering the courtroom. However, the very attributes that made him such a successful attorney did not serve him well in his marriage. He often treated his wife as if she represented opposing counsel. He was cold, domineering, emotionally restricted, and demanding. Although not physically abusive, he was extremely controlling, and she lived in constant fear of his criticisms. He ran the household as if it was a military base, demanding perfection, orderliness, and cleanliness, except when it came to his cats. His four beloved cats could do no wrong.

His wife often said, "He loves those cats more than he loves me or the children." And she was probably right. He doted over his cats. Each night, when he returned home from his work, he would sit down on his plush leather couch, adorned in his expensive suit, and call for his cats. They would respond by leaping up to his lap, brushing themselves against his body, purring in harmony. As they danced about his lap, he would often give them treats. "My cats are the most precious things in the world," he would say.

So why does a man who is so demanding, so controlling, such a perfectionist, and so emotionally restricted to his family act this way towards his cats? Is it simply because he loves them? It's obvious that he does. But given that he treats his family so differently, does that imply that he really doesn't love his wife and children? What is it about these cats that allow him to behave in this manner? What might exist emotionally in him that motivates him to behave this way?

Let's take each of these questions separately.

What is it about these cats that allow him to behave in this manner? Perhaps it has to do with how loving these cats are towards him. What's interesting about this aspect of the equation is that many pet-loving people are not particularly drawn to cats; they prefer dogs. They claim that cats are much more independent and more aloof than dogs. These pet owners want a pet that essentially worships them, a pet whose world is oriented to please its master. Cats can be very loving, and I'm sure that this is part of the equation, but not the lion's share.

What might exist emotionally in him that motivates him to behave this way towards his cats? A likely answer to this question is that he needs to "feel" love, and his cats allow him to both feel and express his love. When he is loving towards his cats, he feels warm and openhearted. When he gives his love, he is more present in the moment and less tied up in his rational mind, the place in which he spends most of his time. Furthermore, the more he *cannot* give his love to his fellow human beings, the more he needs his pets to feel and express his love.

So why can he give his love to his pets and not to his family? The answer may be because his pets are nonthreatening. There are no perceived threats emanating from his pets. There are no power struggles between him and his pets. He can be vulnerable with his pets and lower his shields to let his energy out.

There probably was a time, early in his relationship with his wife, in which he could occasionally lower his shields, be vulnerable with her, and give her the loving energy he holds in his body. Unfortunately, those days have long passed. That doesn't mean that they cannot return. He obviously has the ability to love. He simply has to open his heart to the people who share his world.

Unfortunately, this is not an atypical scenario. There are many people who can express their love to their pets and not to their fellow human beings. Sadly, there are those who have never been able to develop an intimate relationship and express their love within a relationship. There are also those who have developed intimate relations in which they were able to give their love, but over time they have closed that flow of energy. Most often, this is a result of a perceived emotional injury in which either one or both parties in the relationship feels emotionally violated. This may develop as a result of a single event or an ongoing experience of emotional attack or consistent, frequent conflict. It can also be the result of a passive process in which one or both members of the relationship withdraw emotionally from the other. In either case, the end result is a shutdown of the flow of loving energy within the relationship. The cost is not only to the relationship. The cost is to the individual who has limited their access to feel love and express love in the world, therefore limiting their life experience as a human being.

Depression and Giving

It is interesting to discuss depression in the context of giving, because, in effect, the emotional state of depression is the antithesis of the emotional state of giving. Depression is an internally focused mode, one that is restricting energy. It is narcissistically oriented. By this I mean that the emotional state of depression is extremely self-centered. The depressed person is essentially obsessed by his or her own feelings and thoughts and is continually evaluating, internally commenting on, and judging these thoughts and feelings. Depression is directed toward the self, not toward the other. It is directly opposed to the emotional state of giving.

Giving, on the other hand, is an outwardly focused mode in which an individual is expressing and expending energy toward someone or something else. Focus is directed towards the outside world.

Depression restricts energy. It's as if the "shields" are always up. Depression uses a great deal of energy. However, this energy is used to contain and not expand. It is an energy turned inward. This is why fatigue is a common symptom of the depressed person. Fatigue results from the amount of energy being used to contain the underlying issues of depression.

Freud theorized that depression is a result of "anger turned inward," and the containment of this anger uses a substantial amount of energy. In a manner of speaking, depression is self-indulgent, the focus continually within. It's as if we have taken a vacation from the outside world, and not a good vacation at that. It is a state of emotional wounding, and often when an animal is wounded, it retreats. Life's challenges, burdens, and disappointments can be overwhelming at times, and sometimes all we would like to do is retreat. Depression is an emotional retreat.

Giving is expansive. It is an advancement of life. It is a manifestation of compassion. Compassion is an outwardly focused process. Compassion can be defined as "a feeling of deep sympathy and sorrow for another who is stricken by misfortune, accompanied by a strong desire to alleviate the suffering." If we analyze this definition, we see an outward focus. The word "sympathy," meaning "the power of sharing the feelings of another," is coupled with the desire to relieve the suffering of another. This is the direct opposite of depression.

Therefore, a wonderful way to help alleviate depression is giving.

Taking and Giving

For many of us, the act of giving is difficult. We often assume that this difficulty stems from a lack of available resources. This is usually not the case. More often, a lack of giving, whether monetarily or emotionally, is related to our psychological makeup. We have discussed what it means to be emotionally "tight," or to be very stingy with our emotional energy. When we are oriented in this manner, giving is very difficult.

What about when we aren't emotionally tight—when, in fact, our emotional orientation is warm and appears generous? Does this orientation suggest that the act of giving is not difficult? Not necessarily. We may be more oriented to the world as a "taker." Our worldview may start from the position of "what's in it for me," which of course is a view that is the direct opposite of giving. We may be very charming and fun loving, but also manipulative.

Let's look at the psychological dynamics of being oriented as a "taker." Paradoxically, we may often believe that we will be taken from or exploited in some manner, and as a result, we can be self-protective and a bit paranoid. We are often highly alert and quite good at sizing up a situation. We tend to be opportunistic, evaluating a situation from the vantage point of how it might benefit us. What is particularly interesting is that we are often highly successful, accumulate much wealth, and actually have a lot to give.

When we operate from the place of the "taker," our first response to a request is often "no." However, after we have had time to process the request, we often change our position and may actually give more than asked. This is an important dynamic that is worth exploring. When the initial request is made, we respond from a position of being taken from. Having been requested from, we are not in a position of control; we are not the requester. Over time, however, we may relax our guard, rationally consider the request, and then proceed from a place of giving. Now we become the giver and therefore are in control of the situation. It is significant to note that we actually make a psychological shift from a position of protecting ourselves, for fear of being taken from, to a position of openness in which we are now able to give. The more open we are, the more able we are to give.

How is this process different when we are operating from the mode of "taker" and we initiate the giving? This can be an interesting process. As long as our gift is received well and appropriately acknowledged, all is well. Recall how our savior of the monastery reacted when the master failed to acknowledge his gift. If we are giving, we often expect a certain degree of acknowledgment, even when we are participating in a role we should be fulfilling. For example, as fathers we often want acknowledgment from our wife when we act as fathers should act.

Sometimes our reactions can be extreme when we feel that we have extended ourselves and the person to whom we have extended has not properly accepted our generosity. Consider the following scenario. I was working with a young male client, John, who was seventeen years old. He had recently obtained his driver's license and was very excited about this accomplishment. John had an uncle whom he described as very wealthy and "bigger than life."

The uncle had been divorced for many years. Recently the uncle bought a new high-end Mercedes Benz automobile that became his pride and joy. John received an invitation to attend a family wedding. The wedding was to be held in a lovely countryside mansion about two hours' drive from the city. His entire family had been invited to the wedding, and he was looking forward to reconnecting with his many cousins who were similar in age.

A few of the cousins contacted John to make arrangements to drive to the wedding together. They were all excited about this event. Shortly after receiving the invitation, John received a phone call from his uncle. He had always been a bit intimidated by his uncle and usually assumed a compliant posture. The uncle boasted about his beautiful new car and all the features that it had. He then said that, although he lets no one even touch the car, he decided to make an exception and let John accompany him to the wedding and let him drive the car "the whole way." This information was received with utter silence.

John didn't know what to do. He didn't want to offend his uncle, but he had already made a prior commitment to drive to the wedding with his cousins. Sheepishly, he told his uncle about his travel arrangements with his cousins. "No problem, boy; just tell them you changed your mind and you'll be driving your uncle's brand-new Mercedes," the uncle said. Once again, there was silence on the phone. Finally my client said in a very deferential voice, "I really appreciate your offer and I would love to drive with you in your new car, but I would really like to drive with my cousins. I haven't seen them for a long time, and we were all looking forward to driving up together. You understand?" Once again, there was silence on the phone. Then, in a rather loud and angry voice, my client heard, "You mean to tell me that you would rather drive up with that lot, who never even call you, than me? After all I've done for you, this is how you treat me? Well, you can forget that I ever even called, and don't bother saying 'hello' at the wedding." The uncle slammed down the phone, leaving my client feeling terrible about the whole encounter.

My client and I worked on this phone call for several sessions. It was difficult for John not to feel guilty and ashamed that somehow he had let his uncle down.

Unfortunately this type of interaction is not such an uncommon occurrence. From the uncle's vantage point, he was extending himself, giving himself to his nephew and actually doing him a favor by allowing him to drive with him to the wedding and drive his brand-new car. The uncle felt that his offer was a gift, a privilege. Regardless of the circumstances, he felt rejected by his nephew and reacted in anger and withdrawal. When the giver does not feel well received, the reaction is often anger and even rage. The giver feels hurt and rejected, and this experience can be magnified if they perceive the recipient as being below them in status. As far as the uncle was concerned, he was rejected by a lowly teenage boy.

This process is not conscious. It is reactive and indicative of a high level of entitlement and insecurity. Only through awareness and an empathetic understanding of the other person's position can this type of behavior be changed.

> *Do not stand on a high pedestal and take five cents in your hand and say, "Here, my poor man," but be grateful that the poor man is there, so by making a gift to him you are able to help yourself. It is not the receiver that is blessed, but it is the giver. Be thankful that you are allowed to exercise your power of benevolence and mercy in the world, and thus become pure and perfect.*
>
> Indian spiritual leader Swami Vivekananda[33]

The Mindful Way: Giving

For one day, make a concerted effort to increase your awareness of giving. Hold an intention to give in as many ways as possible. Be aware of the many opportunities that present themselves during the day in which you can give. Allow your awareness to envelop the little ways in which you can bestow a simple act of kindness: perhaps holding a door open for someone, welcoming the car that is trying to change lanes in front of you, or picking up a piece of trash that was not yours and depositing it in a trash can. During this one day, orient yourself to helping others.

At the end of the day, reflect on the ways in which you gave of yourself. Write down as many of these moments as you can recall. Then close your eyes and concentrate on your breathing for a while. Bring your awareness to the ways in which you gave during the day. How does it feel? Where in your body do you feel the sensation? What color is it? Just sit with your experience. When you are ready, simply open your eyes.

Consider committing to two days of this "giving practice" and eventually adding additional days.

Chapter Seventeen

The Story of Nachiketa: Identity

Nachiketa was the son of a wealthy businessman. His father, desiring to secure a place in heaven, decided to make a significant gift to the Brahmins, the local priests. He owned a large herd of cattle and pledged to gift a significant portion to the priests. The father, wanting to make his contribution in ceremonious fashion, established a day when he would invite the priests to receive his gift and publicly make his donation. On that day, the priest attended the ceremony, which was a glorious affair. After a wonderful feast, the father rose and motioned to his helpers to bring in the cattle that had been designated for donation. Nachiketa, a young boy at the time, stood next to his father and watched the ceremony unfold. As the cattle were brought to the priest, Nachiketa noticed that his father had selected the oldest and weakest cows from his herd. He wondered how worthy a contribution this actually was and questioned his father publicly: "Father, after you have given away all these old cows, to whom might you choose to offer me as sacrificial offering?" Outraged by his son's question, the father answered, "To Yama, the God of Death, shall I offer you as sacrifice-offering!"

Given that these words had been spoken during a hallowed ritual, the father had doomed his son to face death. Nachiketa journeyed to the Kingdom of Yama, the Lord of Death. Upon his arrival, he was told that Yama was not there, that he was attending to serious business. Nachiketa was told that if he wished to see Yama, he must wait. For three days and nights Nachiketa waited without food, water, or shelter. Upon his return, Yama was told of the young boy's presence. Ashamed that no hospitality was offered the boy, Yama went straight to him and apologized for his household's neglect. After all, Nachiketa was a guest in his kingdom and deserved to be treated as such. To appease the boy and atone for the lack of hospitality, Yama offered Nachiketa three boons (wishes), one for each night the boy endured his wait.

For his first boon, Nachiketa asked that his father's anger towards him be soothed and that he, Nachiketa, would be returned to his father's good graces. Nachiketa's wish was motivated by his desire that his father not be burdened by the anger he carried. Yama, pleased by the boy's request, granted his wish.

For his second boon, Nachiketa asked for the wisdom required for him to lead a spiritual life that would contribute to his well-being for the remainder of his life. Yama was again pleased with the boy's request, and so too, the second boon was granted.

Finally Nachiketa asked Yama for his third boon. Nachiketa said, "There is great mystery of what happens to someone after death. Some say that you still exist, and others say not. This great doubt I ask you to resolve."

Yama was taken aback by Nachiketa's request. He tried to discourage the boy from requesting this boon. He explained that this mystery even haunted the gods of old and that the secret of death is hard to know.

But Nachiketa was determined and said to Yama, "I can have no greater teacher than you to teach me this."

Yama pleaded with Nachiketa to ask for another boon. He said, "Ask for sons and grandsons who live a hundred years. Ask for herds of cattle, elephants and horses, gold and vast land. Ask to live as long as you desire. Ask for beautiful women of loveliness rarely seen on earth, riding in chariots, skilled in music and dance to attend to you. But Nachiketa, please, don't ask me about the one thing that is forbidden to men, the secret of death." But Nachiketa was determined to gain this knowledge. He said to Yama, "These pleasures last but until tomorrow, and they wear out the vital powers of life, too. How fleeting is all life on earth! Therefore, keep your horses and chariots, dancing women and music for yourself. Never can mortals be made happy with these. How can we be desirous of wealth when we see your face and know we cannot live while you, O Death, are here? This is the boon I choose and ask you for."

Yama, impressed with the boy's insight, fortitude, and unyielding desire to pursue this question despite having been offered every temptation he could think of, finally yielded to Nachiketa's wish. Yama said, "There are two paths open to men: the wise choose the good and realize the True Self; the foolish choose the path of pleasure leading to a never-ending cycle of birth and death." Yama then explained the nature of the True Self, commenting that when one dies, the body perishes, but not the True Self. He said, "The True Self is never born, nor does it die; it has always been and will always be." He continued by saying that the purpose of life is to realize the True Self. "But how does one realize the True Self?" asked Nachiketa. Yama responded by saying, "Each day, ask yourself the following question: 'Is this who I am?' The answer to the mystery will be known to you eventually." And with these words, Yama disappeared.[34]

I have contemplated this story for many hours. It has led me to think about the question, "Is this who I am?" What a powerful question. Who are we really?

Who Are We?

Are we our thoughts? Well, they are our thoughts, so certainly they must define us in some way. But how reliable are they? We think many things, and the sum total of our thoughts in just a single day is immeasurable. However, our thoughts can be deceptive. Just because we have a thought doesn't mean that the thought accurately depicts the reality of either ourselves or our environment. Often it doesn't. Remember the study in which subjects were asked to do a taste test involving yogurt? By simply thinking that the vanilla yogurt was strawberry flavored, our brain was convinced to taste strawberry. Incredible!

Are we our feelings? Once again, they are our feelings, so how we feel is an essential part of who we are. But our feelings are subject to change at any given moment, and they do seem to change constantly throughout a day, even if the change is only slight. Remember how thoughts affect feelings. One type of thought can generate a completely different feeling than you were experiencing just prior to that thought.

Are we our physical being? Well, it is our body, so how can this not be who we are? Of course our physical being is a part of who we are. However, our physical being is constantly changing. And even our physical being can be misperceived. In the extreme, such as the mental disorder anorexia nervosa, an individual will significantly misidentify their body configuration. People suffering from anorexia believe themselves, and actually visualize themselves, overweight, despite clear, concrete evidence to the contrary. This is a very serious disorder, because the individual's self-concept, that of being overweight, motivates them not to eat an appropriate amount of calories.

Are we our social, cultural, and religious beliefs? Clearly we are influenced by all of these factors. One simply has to view the differences in attitudes, behaviors, customs, and religious practices throughout the world to see how these factors influence who we are. Throughout time, wars have been fought in the name of preserving these aspects of who we see ourselves to be.

So if we see ourselves as being a culmination of all of the above: thoughts; feelings; physical beings; and social, cultural, and religious beliefs; where does that leave us? One place that it leaves us may be illuminated by the definition of what we call "personality." When social science grapples with the question of "who we are," it often looks to concepts such as personality and temperament in an attempt to answer this question.

Personality

The definition of personality includes "the sum total of the physical, mental, emotional, and social characteristics of an individual." Other definitions are "the organized pattern of behavioral characteristics of the individual" and "the essential character of a person." What is interesting is the origin of the word "personality." It comes from the Latin word *persona*, which means mask or character in a play. In ancient theatre, actors wore masks *not* to hide their identities, but rather to convey a particular type of identity reflecting the character they were playing.

Persona and Shadow

Carl Jung, the eminent Swiss psychiatrist, constructed a theory of personality that included the concepts of "persona" and "shadow." Jung theorized that we all maintain a persona, which is our presentation to the world. Conceptually, our persona is the mask we wear that represents what we need to project to the world. It includes our social behavior and our individual style of expressing ourselves. Jung called the persona the "conformity archetype," because it is designed to protect our "ego" by allowing us to behave in a manner that conforms to cultural and societal rules.

In contrast to persona is the concept of "shadow." Shadow houses our dark side, the part of us with which we are uncomfortable or ashamed. The shadow contains our animal instincts, as well as our repressed feelings, and is comprised of behavioral tendencies deemed to be negative. The shadow lurks beneath the surface and can cause us a great deal of pain by "projecting" these feelings onto the world, which in turn causes us to react negatively to the object to which we have projected. In other words, we project, or place, our own shadow feelings onto other people and onto the world. This influences our worldview and our view of other people. The more conscious and mindful we become of our shadow, the better able we are to integrate our shadow with our persona. This process lessens the power and influence of our shadow. We need our shadow side. Jung considered the shadow to be the seat of our creativity.

The relationship between our persona and our shadow may be illustrated in the following story based on an episode of *Star Trek*.

Captain Kirk was dealing with a very difficult experience. An invisible alien life form had entered the starship and decided that Captain Kirk would be a marvelous host during its visit. The effect this alien life form had on Kirk was to split him into two identical beings, two Kirks. However, although each Kirk was an exact replica of the other, they differed in one fundamental way. One Kirk had its "shadow" side removed, leaving this Kirk to be conventional, passive, and conforming. The other Kirk had its "persona" side removed, leaving this Kirk to be aggressive, impulsive, and uncaring. Throughout the episode, the two Kirks demonstrated behavior consistent with their dominant side. The shadow Kirk was unscrupulous, taking what he wanted when he wanted it. He engaged in a number of antisocial-type behaviors, including unwanted advances towards women. He was constantly being rebuffed, and security officers found themselves in a bind trying to deal with their superior officer, who was being accused of unruly behavior. Of course, this Kirk simply lied his way out of each situation and blamed his accuser of falsifying the facts.

Meanwhile, the persona-dominated Kirk was acting in a very tentative manner. He had tremendous trouble maintaining his leadership role as the ship's captain. He couldn't make a decision, regardless of its simplicity. The demands on him became overwhelming, and he withdrew to his quarters to hide from his responsibilities.

Eventually a crisis required the captain to give specific orders that would prevent the annihilation of the ship. Both Kirks appeared on the "bridge" (the central location where the ship is managed). The shadow Kirk barked out orders to the crew that were clearly ineffective, given the situation. Filled with anxiety, the crew hesitated and chose not to follow their commander's directives. All eyes rested on the persona Kirk, waiting for him to respond appropriately. Outraged by the crew's disregard for his orders and the attention given to the persona Kirk, the shadow Kirk attacked his duplicate. When physical contact was made between the two Kirks, an energy field was created. The energy of the shadow was fighting with the energy of the persona, each flowing into the other. Finally, the shadow energy and the persona energy became one, and the two Kirks blended together, restoring a single Kirk whose persona and shadow was fully integrated. After a moment of rebalancing, the "real" Captain Kirk gave the orders necessary to avert disaster.

We indeed need both our shadow energy and our persona energy to function well.

Personality Types

Throughout the centuries, in an attempt to understand who we are, we have been beset by the need to comprehend and categorize personality. As a result, various categories of personality have been developed. These categories, or "types," have been influenced by specific underlying psychological theories. Each theory developed different ways to understand the nature of personality. Categorizing personality is meant to convey a specific set of behaviors, thoughts, and feelings that are associated with a specific type of personality. Each type is consistent with these sets of behaviors, thoughts, and feelings. In essence, personality types have been developed to reflect and categorize the essential character of different types of individuals. Some of these theories are complex, while others are more fundamental. All seem to have been established to give us a sense of permanence.

"Type A" Personality versus "Type B" Personality

One categorization of personality, with which many of us are familiar, categorizes personality as either a "Type A" personality or a "Type B" personality. People with a Type A personality are said to be generally more "uptight." They are characterized as being high achievers, workaholic, impatient, time-conscious, controlling, status seekers, competitive, ambitious, businesslike, and aggressive; and they have difficulty relaxing. People with a Type B personality are said to be more "laid back." They are easygoing, slower paced, relaxed, patient, and not driven by success or status.

Although considered to be a simplistic model of personality, it does illuminate a substantial difference describing who we are in the world.

The Myers-Briggs Type Indicator

A popular personality type instrument is the Myers-Briggs Type Indicator, which is based on Carl Jung's psychological types, developed in 1921. The Myers-Briggs test identifies sixteen personality types based on personality preferences. Jung theorized that there are four main functions of consciousness: Sensation and Intuition, which are "perceiving" functions; and Thinking and Feeling, which are "judging" functions. Each can be influenced by what he called "attitude types," which are either extraversion (action-oriented people) or introversion (people who are more reflective). Each of the sixteen personality types are a specific combination of these variables.

The Enneagram

The Enneagram is another model of personality. It describes nine prominent personality types. Each type has specific characteristics that reflect our inborn temperament, as well as the influence that childhood factors have had on the overall development of our personality. Each type expresses a pattern of thinking and emotions and is considered to be our dominant personality orientation. There is a significant amount of overlay from one personality type to the next.

What is interesting about the Enneagram is that it accounts for how life can impact the functioning of our personality. When we are in an emotionally healthy place, our personality not only functions at its highest capacity (according to the attributes of the specific type) but takes on the positive aspects of a corresponding personality type. However, when we are stressed, our personality not only functions at its lowest capacity (according to the attributes of the specific type) but takes on the negative aspects of a corresponding personality type.

Even traditional psychology recognizes that people under stress are likely to act and feel differently than when they are not under stress. The Rorschach test (commonly known as the "ink blot" test) is a highly respected, highly validated psychological assessment tool used to gain insight about the functioning and inner world of an individual. This test is designed to actually differentiate how an individual is likely to act when stressed and when not stressed.

Buddhist Personality Types

The eminent Buddhist teacher and psychologist Jack Kornfield, in his book *The Wise Heart,* describes three basic temperaments that make up three categories of personality.[35] They are the Greed or Grasping temperament, the Aversive or Angry temperament, and the Deluded or Confused temperament. Each of these has a dominant orientation to the world. Buddhist psychology contends that only through transforming the unhealthy patterns of our dominant personality type can we express our healthy natural temperament.

The Greed or Grasping temperament is based on desire. These individuals are oriented in the world to want more and to seek comfort and pleasure. This can lead to self-centeredness, vanity, pride, jealousy, and willfulness. Once transformed, the Greed or Grasping temperament can evolve into a spirit of generosity and abundance.

The Aversive or Angry temperament is based on judgment and rejection. This temperament finds fault and frequently identifies problems. These individuals are critical, quarrelsome, and easily displeased. This can lead to vindictiveness, anger, hatred, aggression, and the need to control. Once transformed, the Aversive temperament gives rise to wisdom and non-contentiousness and unites opposites.

The Deluded or Confused temperament is based on uncertainty and confusion. Individuals with this temperament do not relate easily to the world and often have a sense of not knowing what to do. This often leads to worry, doubt, anxiety, and negligence. Once transformed, the Deluded temperament gives rise to spaciousness and understanding.

The Diagnostic and Statistical Manual of Mental Disorders (DSM)

Traditional psychology is invested in understanding the nature of personality. In the field of clinical psychology, a diagnostic manual known as the DSM is used to help clinicians define and identify mental disorders. Within the classifications of mental disorders is a section entitled "Personality Disorders." The DSM recognizes that we all have certain personality "traits," which are defined as "enduring patterns of perceiving, relating to, and thinking about the environment and oneself that are exhibited in a wide range of social and personal contexts." What this means is that we all have a combination of traits that make up our personality. However, when these personality traits "are inflexible and maladaptive and cause significant functional impairment," the DSM classifies them as personality disorders.[36]

Temperament

Experts have debated about the fundamental factors that contribute to the development of personality. Some say that purely biological factors based on genetic coding are the essential ingredients of personality (the nature argument). Others say that the development of personality is the result of environmental factors, such as love and nurturance (the nurture argument). Most experts now agree that the development of personality is a combination of both nature and nurture. We do not seem to be born as a blank slate. Rather, we seem to enter this life with an emotional orientation. This emotional orientation is the context in which our personality will develop. This context can be referred to as our temperament. Our temperament will play a significant role in how we behave, how we think, and how we feel.

Temperament has been defined as one's "natural predisposition" and "the combination of mental, physical, and emotional traits of a person." Temperament studies have been conducted for decades, but we are still unclear about how one's temperament is formed.

Temperament appears to be the landscape in which our personality develops. Just as only certain plants and vegetation will grow in a rocky, sandy environment, our temperament sets the stage for the development of a personality most consistent with the nature of that temperament. Of course, many other social and environmental factors will affect the development of our personality.

One of the more prominent studies of temperament was a longitudinal study conducted in New York in the 1950s by a team of doctors (Thomas, Chess, Birch, Hertzig, and Korn).[37] What they found was that most babies could be categorized into three groups: easy babies, who were very adaptable, had normal sleeping and eating habits, and were generally happy; difficult babies, who cried often, were fussy, irritable, very emotional, and had irregular sleeping and eating habits; and slow-to-warm-up babies, who were slow to adapt, tended to withdraw from new situations, and had a low activity level.

Their findings are most helpful when we translate them into real-world situations. In the spirit of equality and fairness, parents often believe that all children should be raised in the same manner. However, given that children have different temperaments, using the same child-rearing approach may not result in a happy, well-developed child or a harmonious family life. Adjusting one's parenting style to the needs and temperament of a child will benefit both child and parent. It is very helpful for parents to have an understanding of their child's temperament. However, the assessment of a child's temperament is not something that is routinely done.

When my daughter was just an infant, we were invited to participate in a temperament study. It involved answering a rather lengthy series of questions regarding how we viewed my daughter's behavioral attributes. I was a little suspect about the study and wondered how accurate a profile could be, based solely on parental observation and feedback. After the questionnaire was completed, our answers were combined and tabulated and a temperament profile was developed. I remember receiving this document in the mail and opening it with some skepticism. To my amazement, everything stated in the temperament profile fit my daughter to a tee. What was particularly helpful was our ability to develop a child-rearing approach that was based on her temperament. She was not an easy baby, but being aware of her temperament was definitely helpful— and still is.

Legacy

Legacy is defined as "anything handed down from the past, as from an ancestor or predecessor." All too often we overlook the power of legacy. How can we not have been influenced by the past? How could we not have been influenced by the travails of our ancestors? We tend not to give legacy the credence it deserves, because often its influence is not necessarily conscious. We may believe that something that occurred several decades ago doesn't influence our daily life or present way of functioning, but this is simply a form of denial. If you are an African American, you have been emotionally influenced by the history of slavery in America. That influence plays a role in your present identity. If you are Jewish, a history of persecution, culminating in the Holocaust, plays a role in your present identity. We have all been influenced by our ancestry.

Sometimes we are influenced without even knowing the historic facts that have influenced us. Erik Erikson, the famous psychologist who developed the concept of "identity crisis," is a perfect example of this. Erik's mother was Jewish. However, his biological father was not. He was Danish. He was raised Jewish by his mother and his non-biological father, who was also Jewish. The circumstance of his birth and his lineage was never revealed to Erik. Later in life, in published works, Erikson revealed that ever since he was a young boy he felt uneasy, out of place, and unsure of his own identity. Eventually, as an adult, the truth of his birth was revealed to him.

In the book *The Art of Happiness*, the Dalai Lama comments on the influence of past experience on current behavior. He states that Western belief is constrained by the perspective that everything can be explained within a single lifetime, as opposed to Buddhist thought, which believes in the concept of rebirth and multiple lifetimes. Buddhism contends that prior life experience results in a karmic influence that affects our current life experience. He further asserts that Buddhism supports the idea of "dispositions and imprints."[38] He explains that certain events that occur earlier in one's life can leave an imprint on the mind and influence a person's behavior later on in life. The concept of dispositions and imprints is similar to the Western notion of the unconscious and its influence on individual functioning. Consistent with Buddhist belief, he contends that these imprints can be carried over from previous lifetimes.

Whether one believes in past lives, karma, or Jung's collective unconscious, it's obvious that the past can have a very powerful influence on the present. Our history influences how we feel, how we think, and ultimately who we believe ourselves to be. It shapes our identity. Our national, cultural, religious, and individual identity is formed in large measure by our legacy.

Either denial of or attachment to the influence of our legacy can entrap us. If we deny the influence of a traumatic event, past or present, we can never heal the trauma and it will continue to have a hold on us. If we strongly attach to a traumatic event, we can develop a victim identity that can continually shape how we see the world, how we operate in the world, and how we feel about ourselves. Either extreme does not promote emotional well-being. When we are able to acknowledge the influences of the past, whether from our immediate family of origin or our ancestral heritage, we can begin to develop an awareness that can allow us to detach from these elements that have exercised power over our life. And through this detachment, we can significantly change our worldview and ultimately how we function in the world.

Compensating

We have all developed ways to cope with reality and combat our anxiety. Some of us use denial; some use anger; some use aversion; some use grandiosity; some use all possible methods. The list can go on and on. The point is that we tend to engage in behaviors and thoughts that are designed to make us feel more secure. The problem arises when these tactics are not helpful and may be harmful. A person can deny the pain caused by placing their hand in a fire, but the hand will still burn and damage will be inflicted.

The more we compensate for our internal insecurity and the more we resist accepting the impermanence of our life (what we resist persists), the more we assure that our insecurity remains. Remember the lock on the closet door designed to keep the ghost at bay? It only assures us that there is something really terrifying that needs to be locked up. The more we try to maintain control over things that are not controllable, the more we suffer. Despite all our efforts to understand and categorize who we are, we are simply more than just our personality, our thoughts and feelings, and our heritage. The next chapter will address our true nature.

> *God grant me the serenity to accept the things I cannot change; courage to change the things I can; and wisdom to know the difference.*
>
> The Serenity Prayer

The Mindful Way: Who Am I?

- Close your eyes. Begin mindful breathing. Be aware of breathing in and breathing out—just rest your awareness there.
- Now shift your awareness and ask yourself the following question: "Who am I?"
- Open your eyes and respond by either saying your response aloud or writing it down.
- Close your eyes again, take a few breaths, and ask the question again: "Who am I?"
- Repeat this process for ten minutes.
- How did your responses change? How did they progress? What insight and awareness can this offer you?

Our True Nature

In 1957, in an old Buddhist temple in Thailand believed to have been built in the thirteenth century, a miraculous event occurred. The temple housed a ten-foot-high clay Buddha, which had to be moved to a new site. The task of moving the Buddha was daunting, and during the removal operation, things went terribly wrong (or did they?). A large crane was brought to the site to be used to transport the statute. The workmen fastened their ropes to the Buddha and ordered the crane to lift the statue. The crane lifted the Buddha from the spot in which it sat and began to move it outside of the temple. Just then a resounding "crack" was heard, as the boom of the crane snapped. The statue crashed to the ground, opening a crack in the clay Buddha. Just then it began to rain, and the workers decided to stop work for the day. The Buddha sat in the developing mud.

That night, the head monk of the temple had a powerful dream that revealed to him that the Buddha statue embodied divine illumination. He woke early in the morning with an intense curiosity about the meaning of the dream. With flashlight in hand, he hurried to the statue. As he gazed upon the statue, he noticed a glimmer at the point at which the clay had cracked. He quickly began to investigate the spot, using his fingers to enlarge the cracked area. Finally, when the crack had been sufficiently enlarged, he shined his flashlight into the opening. A brilliant ray shone from the Buddha. This increased the monk's desire to unveil the secret of the Buddha. With renewed energy, he chipped away at the Buddha's outer crust until he had created a gaping hole in the clay.

By now several monks had arrived at the site, watching this activity. The head monk stopped his work, stepped back from the Buddha, and shined his light once again. This time there was no mistaking what he had discovered. The Buddha was made of pure gold. As the gold reflected the monk's light beam, he turned to his fellow monks and said, "Beneath the outer surface the Buddha is pure and illuminated; so too are we."

Today, the five-ton, solid-gold Buddha resides in a temple in Thailand known as the Temple of the Golden Buddha. Remnants of the clay that encrusted the Buddha are on display as well. Apparently the Buddha statue was encased in clay centuries ago to hide its value when the monks believed they were about to be invaded by the Burmese.

This story has been told across the universe. It has become a symbol of what is referred to as our true nature or Buddha nature: our pure, immortal, illuminated being, capable of awakening and becoming enlightened.

You Are Who You Have Always Been

In the spirit of knowing who we are, the story of the Golden Buddha presents a powerful metaphor. Do we metaphorically possess a clay shell, and if so, why has it developed? If we think back to the level of vulnerability we all had entering this life, and the continued vulnerability we feel as a result of "the catch," it's only natural to expect that we would build a hardened outer shell to protect ourselves. This shell doesn't come in the form of an outer layer of clay. Rather it comes in the form of our defense mechanisms, which are integrated into our personality. Our beliefs, our constructs, and even our values are developed to protect us. All are in the service of making us feel more secure. We define our world. We create guidelines and rules and beliefs to live by, and then we aspire to live by them. These are good ways to be in the world. Every major religion has developed guidelines to help us navigate our way through our life's journey: "Thou shall not kill," "Thou shall not steal," etc.

When we fail to live up to our guidelines, we often feel bad. At times we even feel bad when we have lived up to them, wondering, "What is the meaning of life?" We are in a constant struggle to control our environment, to make life predictable, so we can feel safe. However, it's like trying to hold sand in our clenched fist. Regardless how hard we press, the sand still sifts through our fingers. We cannot control that which is impermanent, that which is destined to change. We can only learn to live with and accept "the deal." Only when we open our hearts and feel compassion for ourselves, our fellow human beings, our earth, and all that occupies it can we begin to realize our true strength, our true nature, our loving essence.

Pure Essence

Beneath our constructed self (some call it our "egoic self," "egoic mind," or "ordinary mind") is our true nature. According to some of our most venerated spiritual leaders, such as the Dalai Lama, our nature is pure, loving, compassionate, and gentle. This view is in direct opposition to some of the Western world's most revered psychological theorists, such as Freud, who viewed the human animal as instinctual and aggressive in nature.

How we choose to view our nature matters. Studies have repeatedly shown that when we are exposed to violence and aggression, we are more apt to be "primed" for more aggressive behavior. If we identify ourselves as having an aggressive nature, we will establish the conditions and the mindset to be aggressive. If we believe that by nature we are gentle beings, we will be better able to bring our gentleness to the forefront.

The Ordinary Mind and the Natural Mind

Our purity of nature lies beneath the ordinary mind or egoic self. The ordinary mind is dualistic, driven by our ego, and is the *relative mind*. The ordinary mind creates our sense of self. It is our thoughts, feelings, memories, constructs, and interpretations of our world, and it is driven by our unconscious. The ordinary mind has been referred to as "that which possesses discriminating awareness, that which possesses a sense of duality, which grasps or rejects something external…"[39]

The ordinary mind is influenced by variables such as culture, family, ethnicity, religion, and past experience. It defines who we are and how we think about ourselves. It is our story. It creates an "I-ness" and contributes to the feeling of being separate from others and not interconnected. It is "…the mind that thinks, plots, desires, manipulates, that flares up in anger, that creates and indulges in waves of negative emotions and thoughts, that has to go on and on asserting, validating, and confirming its existence by fragmenting, conceptualizing, and solidifying experience."[40]

Metaphorically, the ordinary mind is represented as a candle flame subject to the winds of circumstance, or as the surface of the ocean, subjected to continuous environmental forces. When the wind is calm, the flame or ocean surface is calm; when blustery it becomes agitated. It is in a constant state of flux, solely dependent on environmental factors. It contains our most destructive and negative emotions.

Consider how egocentric we have always been and how this is driven by our ego-centered mind. In the seventeenth century, Galileo, referred to as "the Father of Modern Science," was publicly denounced and subjected to the Roman Inquisition because of his support of Copernicus, who had theorized nearly one hundred years earlier that the sun, not the earth, was the center of the universe. He was condemned by the Catholic Church for heresy and placed under house arrest for the remainder of his life. This action was a direct result of the needs of the powers at large to maintain their attachment to the concept that everything revolved around the Earth. The Earth was the most significant planet in the universe and, by extension, so were its inhabitants.

In contrast to the ordinary mind is our untainted mind, or what has been referred to as our natural mind or, in ancient Buddhist texts, as the "primordial mind." The primordial mind has been described as "unsullied and unadorned, devoid of center and boundaries, in its emptiness and radiance."[41] It is our essence, untouched by change or death. It is our true nature or our soul. Unlike the ordinary mind, it is not driven by clinging and desire, attachment, aversion, or fear. It is the pure non-dualistic mind, or as I refer to it, the *mind of absolute awareness*. It is obscured by our ordinary mind as is the sun on a cloudy day. It is boundless and encompasses the basic virtues of loving-kindness, compassion, joy, and equanimity. These virtues counteract our most fundamental negative emotions: loving-kindness counteracts hatred and anger; compassion counteracts attachment; joy counteracts envy; and equanimity counteracts pride.

Whether we believe in an ordinary mind or a natural mind is not the essential issue. The issue is that beneath our defense mechanisms, beneath our fear and anxiety, beneath our grandiosity or self-loathing, beneath our pride, and beneath our strong identification of who we are lies our true nature. Our true nature is untainted by our worldly experience and is loving, caring, and calm. It has always been there. It never left us. Only the forces of our environment, the forces of fear and anxiety, have moved us away from residing in our true nature.

O Nobly Born, O you of glorious origins, remember your radiant true nature, the essence of mind. Trust it. Return to it. It is home.
The Tibetan Book of the Dead[42]

Separateness versus Interconnectedness

Our ego-driven mind helps us define and organize our world. Its development is essential to our functioning and well-being. It instructs us how we should conduct ourselves, how we should think and feel about things, and who we should strive to be. It is based in a paradigm of duality: I-you, us-them, subject-object. It develops our concept of self and gives us a sense of identity and how we fit into the world. It motivates us to seek affiliation and connect to others in our world. However, the desire to affiliate can cause much grief and suffering.

Consider the following question. What is the difference between a lion and a tiger? Obviously there are many answers to this question. Although they are both large cats, they look different, live in different regions of the world, and have other differences. One such difference, however, is very significant: their social structure. Tigers lead a very solitary life. They are loners. In fact, after mating, a male tiger will abandon its mate and actually kill its male offspring later on if encountered in its territory. In contrast, lions lead a very social lifestyle; they affiliate. They live in prides, and their social order is highly defined and crucial to their existence. I often see emotional problems and anguish in individuals leading a solitary life, a tiger existence, when in fact they wish to lead a more socially connected life, a lion's lifestyle, which is more in keeping with our developmental history.

The dual nature of the ego-driven mind supports attachment to things, concepts, people, and beliefs. However, those very things we are attached to are transient in nature. They are constantly evolving, changing, and decaying and, as a result, can contribute to feelings of separateness and a yearning to belong.

We are not truly separate. We are all interconnected. Consider the highly popular film *Avatar*. *Avatar* is the story of the Na'vi, a tribal group of blue-skinned beings who live in complete harmony with their environment. Their planet is rich in a very valuable mineral, and the US government wants to excavate the mineral for its own use. In an attempt to avoid using force as a first option, a soldier is sent to the planet to infiltrate the Na'vi, learn their ways, and convince them to relocate, leaving the mineral deposit available for excavation. Through a chance encounter, when the soldier is fighting for his life against the predators of the jungle, he meets a Na'vi woman, the daughter of the tribe's spiritual leader, who saves his life. She expresses outrage that she had to kill these predators to save his life, but she recognizes signs from Eywa, their deity who keeps their ecosystem in perfect equilibrium, that he is a special being. She brings the solider to her tribe, and he learns the way of the Na'vi.

Eywa provides a connecting link through a biological system of interconnectedness between all living organisms on the planet. All living beings are part of a collective consciousness of the planet. As a result, the Na'vi have the ability to tap into this consciousness and communicate telepathically, receive and input memories, and use their psychic abilities to communicate with their ancestors.

Sounds farfetched? Perhaps, but many would argue that we are all interconnected in this way.

Let's take a practical view of interconnectedness. If you're reading a print copy of this book, think about the page you are reading now. Think about the paper on which the words appear. Consider the process that created the paper: the tree that was felled, the workers who felled the tree, the sun and rain that nourished the tree, the food that was consumed by the workers who felled the tree, the workers who grew the food, etc., etc. Clearly, as we consider this process, it becomes apparent that everything is interconnected. Yet many of us feel so isolated, so disconnected. Why is that? Our feelings of isolation and disconnection are the byproduct of an ego-driven mind. We are oriented to be individuals and to maintain a separate identity. But in so doing we often close our hearts to the rest of the world and feel isolated. We are often competitive, envious, possessive, and nationalistic. These feelings and behaviors help to support an "us versus them" mentality. Yet when we open our hearts, when we feel compassion and empathy for one another, and when we recognize that we all suffer the travails of life, we can feel connected to one another. If you were ever part of a natural disaster or a traumatic event that affected your entire community, such as an earthquake or the tragedy of 9/11, you likely experienced this sense of connectedness.

Despite a lifetime of experience, our true essence never changes. We become more and more layered. The common metaphor in psychotherapy is the peeling of the onion, removing each layer to reach the core of who we are. We may have changed dramatically in the way we look, or in the way we present to the world, or even the way we feel about our self. And this can be very positive. But underneath it all, we are all who we have always been: that vulnerable, innocent being seeking security and love, still waiting for the love and attention needed to feel safe and calm in the world.

But something has fundamentally changed. We are no longer the little baby who was completely dependent on the environment to fulfill its needs, to give it love and adoration, and to feed it emotionally and physically as well. We are adults now, and we as adults don't need to rely as heavily on our external environment to get our needs met. We are capable of giving those things to ourselves. We are capable of loving ourselves. We are capable of *not* judging ourselves and casting aspersions on who we are. We are capable of self-regulation and self-soothing. All the things we needed to get from our mothers, we can now give to ourselves. However, we need to believe that we can, and we need to become "aware" so we can.

Contemplation and Meditation

Throughout history and throughout the world, contemplation has been encouraged as a means to cultivate awareness and enhance concentration. Plato, and other philosophers, believed that through contemplation, our soul could ascend to knowledge of the divine and experience union with the "source" (the Force). Prayer and meditation are common contemplation practices.

The word *meditate* comes from the Latin root *meditatum*, to ponder. Meditation is referred to as a contemplative process.

In an article written by Drs. Walsh and Shapiro, meditation is referred to as "a family of self-regulation practices that focus on training attention and awareness in order to bring mental processes under greater voluntary control and thereby foster general mental well-being and development and/or specific capacities such as calm, clarity, and concentration."[43]

Let's take a closer look at this definition. Imbedded in this definition is the concept of self-regulation, or the ability to regulate our emotions. As we discussed earlier, the process of self-regulation is an integral part of emotional well-being and is lacking in infants. Infants do not have the capacity to self-soothe and therefore to self-regulate. They are dependent on the environment to intervene to modify their feelings, their experience. We therefore begin our emotional journey with little to no ability to control our emotions. If we are uncomfortable or distressed, we cry. If not, we don't. Of course, temperament will play a significant role in our experience of discomfort. So a major part of our emotional journey is to learn how to regulate our emotions: how not to be reactive and how to bring calm to ourselves.

Back to the definition. "Self-regulation practices that focus on training attention and awareness." This suggests that the process of meditation, the actual practice of meditation, is designed to train our attention to help us better concentrate and heighten our awareness, or make us more aware. The very process of meditation is a constant refocusing of our attention to one specific thing. For example, it is a common practice of meditation to focus solely on the breath.

However, what happens during meditation is that our mind wanders from the breath. We have a thought, feeling, or an image that draws our attention away from the breath. The moment that we notice this, we have become "aware," aware that we are no longer focused on our breath. We simply recognize that we have wandered. We don't engage the thought or judge that we have wandered. We then refocus on the breath. In so doing, we are training the mind to become aware, and we are strengthening our attention. The effect of this is "to bring mental processes under greater voluntary control." That is to say that the greater our attention and the greater our awareness, the more able we are to control our thoughts and emotions: the very process we were unable to do as an infant.

What is the possible result of this practice? The result is to "foster general mental well-being ...such as calm, clarity, and concentration." The more we are aware of our thoughts and emotions, the more we are able to self-regulate and not simply react to our thoughts and emotions. This in turn leads to greater calm, clarity of thought, and increased concentration: in short, greater emotional well-being.

The practice of meditation is quite straightforward; however, there are a multitude of practices, some of which involve visualizations; chanting; or focus on a mantra, a specific object, or a particular theme, such as compassion.

Perhaps the most fundamental meditative practice is simply focusing attention on the breath. During this practice, the meditator finds a suitable environment, usually a room in one's home, or in a garden, or any other place where distraction will be minimal. The meditator can either sit in a cross-legged position (often known as the lotus position), or on a cushion, or in a chair, maintaining an upright position with the spine straight. The eyes can be shut or partially opened. It is important to maintain an alert mind.

Meditation begins with steady rhythmic breathing, a natural breathing that is not forced. It is often helpful to breathe from one's diaphragm, the lower area of one's belly and not solely from one's chest. Placing a hand on the lower belly can be helpful to feel the pattern of the breathing. The focus of attention is directed to the breath. The meditator focuses on the movement of the breath, monitoring the breath as it enters the nostrils, fills the body, and exits the nostrils. Thoughts, images, feelings, and other distractions will enter the mind. This is not a problem. Simply recognize the experience without engaging the experience. It is often helpful to name the experience: for example, "thought," "thought" or "image," "image." The experience should be witnessed without judgment. The moment the meditator becomes aware that he or she is attending to the experience and not concentrating on the breath is the moment of "awareness." The meditator simply refocuses attention to the breath.

Actually, the process of wandering from attention on the breath to attending to thoughts, feelings, and images trains the mind to become more aware, and strengthens attention by returning to a focus on the breath. In essence, meditation is a mind exercise, one that strengthens concentration and increases awareness. Beginners will often start with a sitting that lasts anywhere from five to fifteen minutes. But as they become more comfortable with the process, the time allotted for each sitting will usually increase. A consistent pattern, such as daily practice conducted at a specified time in a specified place, can be helpful, because routine tends to strengthen the commitment to the practice.

In the End

There are many ways besides meditation to improve self-regulation and increase our awareness of what our mind is doing and how our mind is affecting our feelings and our behavior. The key to emotional well-being is that we become aware of what's going on in our mind, and the mind includes both thoughts and feelings. Through awareness, we can be in greater control of our mind and its impact on our behavior, our thoughts, our beliefs and interpretations, and our feelings. Through awareness, we are no longer on automatic pilot, simply reacting with no consciousness about what we are doing or feeling. When we are mindful, we are aware, we are living in the moment, fully present, not preoccupied with the past or the future. We are able to evaluate and to analyze our thoughts and feelings. We are able to change our perspective and consider a situation from a different vantage point. We are better able to bring forth the very qualities that contribute to our emotional well-being: love, compassion, and understanding, all of which contribute to greater tolerance and therefore less stress and anguish.

Practice compassion. Practice awareness. Know that your true nature is loving and kind. Slow down your life and take a breath. Take several breaths. Reconnect with your body and allow your intuitive being to help you navigate through your world.

As the Dalai Lama said, "The purpose of our life is to seek happiness," and "The greater the level of calmness of our mind, the greater our peace of mind, the greater our ability to enjoy a happy and joyful life."

And in the end the love you take is equal to the love you make.

The Beatles, *Abbey Road*

The Mindful Way: Our True Nature through Loving-Kindness

- Close your eyes. Begin mindful breathing. Be aware of breathing in and breathing out—just rest your awareness there.
- Now shift your awareness and repeat the following to yourself three times:
    - ° May I be filled with loving-kindness.
    - ° May I be safe.
    - ° May I be well in body and mind.
    - ° May I be at ease.
    - ° May I be happy.
- Now change your focus and choose someone you are close to and repeat the following three times:
    - ° May you be filled with loving-kindness.
    - ° May you be safe.
    - ° May you be well in body and mind.
    - ° May you be at ease.
    - ° May you be happy.

- Now change your focus again and extend loving-kindness to others. Repeat the following three times:
  - May you be filled with loving-kindness.
  - May you be safe.
  - May you be well in body and mind.
  - May you be at ease.
  - May you be happy.
- Change your focus and extend loving-kindness to a difficult person in your life. Repeat the following three times:
  - May you be filled with loving-kindness.
  - May you be safe.
  - May you be well in body and mind.
  - May you be at ease.
  - May you be happy.
- Finally, change your focus and picture yourself as a small child. Extend loving-kindness to your inner child. Repeat the following three times:
  - May you be filled with loving-kindness.
  - May you be safe.
  - May you be well in body and mind.
  - May you be at ease.
  - May you be happy.
- Sit with your experience, knowing your true nature from within.
- When you are ready, open your eyes.

Remember: Our true nature is always present.

Notes

Acknowledgments

Although I have sometimes been described as a "dreamer" (and "I'm not the only one"), there have been a few things that I never thought I could accomplish. One has been writing a book, and the other has been running a marathon. Now that I have written a book, which has been a marathon in its own right, I think I'll forgo the running of a marathon. But I could not have done this without the love and support from so many. So I would like to share my gratitude with all of you.

This journey began as an offshoot of a creative, dynamic process: the creation and development of a mindfulness and emotional health workshop. It was born out of an ongoing exploration of the relationship between mindfulness and emotional well-being. Through this process I became inspired to delve more deeply into the topic, which eventually became the writing of this book. I will forever be grateful to my workshop partner, Charlotte, for her encouragement, inspiration, and support.

Along the way, many others held the torch that lit the way for me to continue my journey.

I'm thankful to my friend and colleague Dr. Terry Oleson, who was the first to read through my manuscript and offer comments and edits above and beyond what was expected. In a similar fashion, my friend Dr. Kathy Sheridan responded to my manuscript with such love and enthusiasm, and a whole other set of edits, that I actually began to believe that I could do this. I'm thankful to my gracious sister-in-law

Brenda, who actually has a publishing and editing background, for not only providing "professional" edits, but assuring me that this was a "real" book filled with insights and joy.

Throughout the writing of this book, I continued to deepen my understanding of mindfulness and spirituality in general. None played a greater role in this process than my teacher, colleague, and friend, Jack Kornfield. You are an amazing guide, and I thank you for your wisdom, insight, and humor.

I would also like to thank my publisher, Morgan James, and specifically Rick Frishman and David Hancock, who believed in me and encouraged me to complete this project. Through them I met my amazing editor, Amanda Rooker, whose comments and edits were not only elucidating but heartfelt. Thank you.

And of course, this book could never have been written without the love and support of my close friends, my extended family, and my lovely wife Marsha and children Neisha and Jacob. You have enriched my life and have always supported me to be "me." I am profoundly grateful.

With Love!

About the Author

Neil Kobrin, PhD, is a licensed clinical psychologist with decades of experience in human transformation and emotional well-being. He is the founder and president of the Academy of Mindful Psychology and leads international workshops and retreats in mindfulness and emotional well-being. He is a former university president and psychology graduate school president and has taught doctoral-level psychology for many years. In addition to maintaining a private clinical practice, he provides continuing education and is an executive and educational consultant. He lives with his family in Mill Valley, California, surrounded by the grandeur of the redwoods.

For more information about Dr. Neil Kobrin, his workshops, or the Academy of Mindful Psychology, visit DrNeilKobrin.com.

ACADEMY OF
MINDFUL PSYCHOLOGY

Endnotes

1 Sogyal Rinpoche, Patrick Gaffney, and Andrew Harvey, *The Tibetan Book of Living and Dying* (HarperCollins, 1993), p. 118.

2 Marc Gafni, *The Mystery of Love* (Atria, 2003).

3 Ajahn Chah and Paul Breiter, *Everything Arises, Everything Falls Away: Teachings on Impermanence and the End of Suffering* (Shambhala, 2005).

4 Viktor Frankl, *Man's Search for Meaning* (Washington Square, 1984).

5 All definitions of terms, unless otherwise indicated, are from Dictionary.com.

6 Jon Kabat-Zinn, *Full Catastrophe Living: Using the Wisdom of Your Body and Mind to Face Stress, Pain, and Illness* (Delacorte, 1990).

7 Ruth Baer, "Mindfulness Training as a Clinical Intervention: A Conceptual and Empirical Review," *Clinical Psychology Science Practice* 10 (2003): 125–143.

8 The Dalai Lama and Howard C. Cutler, *The Art of Happiness* (Simon & Schuster, 1999).

9 Martin Luther King Jr., *Strength to Love* (Fortress Press, 1963, reprint 1981), p. 35.

10 Paul R. Fulton and Ronald D. Siegel, "Buddhist and Western Psychology: Seeking Common Ground," in *Mindfulness and Psychotherapy,* ed. Christopher K. Germer, Ronald D. Siegel, and Paul R. Fulton (Guilford Press, 2005), pp. 41–42.

11   "The Gates of Paradise," http://viewonbuddhism.org/resources/zen_
       stories.html, accessed February 2011.

12   "Zen Buddhist Stories—Buddha's World," *Wisdom Quotes, Facts, and
       Articles: Spirituality & Religions on Katinka Hesselink Net*, http://www.
       katinkahesselink.net/tibet/zen-stories.html, accessed September
       2011.

13   Sigmund Freud, *New Introductory Lectures on Psychoanalysis* (Penguin
       Freud Library 2, 1933), pp. 105–10

14   Sigmund Freud, Anna Freud, and James Strachey, *The Essentials of
       Psycho-analysis* (Penguin, 1986), p. 450.

15   Eckhart Tolle, *Stillness Speaks* (Namaste Publications, 2003), p. 27.

16   Jack Kornfield, *After the Ecstasy, the Laundry: How the Heart Grows
       Wise on the Spiritual Path* (Bantam, 2000), p. 74.

17   Malcolm Gladwell, *Blink: The Power of Thinking without Thinking*
       (Little, Brown, 2005), p. 11.

18   Elliot Aronson, *The Social Animal* (Worth, 2011).

19   Dan Siegel, as quoted in Ginger Campbell's "Brain Science Podcast
       #44: Meditation and the Brain with Dan Siegel, MD," http://
       docartemis.com/brain%20science/44-brainscience-Siegel.pdf, p. 14.

20   Shunryū Suzuki and Trudy Dixon, *Zen Mind, Beginner's Mind*
       (Weatherhill, 1970), p. 1.

21   Ron Pogue, "Something More Precious than a Precious Stone,"
       E-piphanies blog, November 11, 2010, http://ronpogue.typepad.
       com/e-piphanies/2010/11/something-more-precious-than-a-
       precious-stone.html, accessed October 2011.

22   Wayne Dyer, BrainyQuote.com, http://www.brainyquote.com/
       quotes/quotes/w/waynedyer154410.html, accessed October 2011.

23   From the Vajrayana Institute, http://www.vajrayana.com.au/
       blog/?p=135, accessed October 2011.

24   Jack Kornfield, *After the Ecstasy, the Laundry: How the Heart Grows
       Wise on the Spiritual Path* (Bantam, 2000), p. 252.

25 Viktor Frankl, *Man's Search for Meaning: An Introduction to Logotherapy* (Simon & Schuster, 1984), p. 92.

26 Daniel J. Siegel, *The Mindful Brain: Reflection and Attunement in the Cultivation of Well-Being* (Norton, 2007), p. 168.

27 "Carl Rogers' Self Theory of Personal Development," available at http://www.scribd.com/doc/28250013/Carl-Rogers-Self-Theory-of-Personality-Development, accessed October 2012.

28 Robert Bornstein and Mary Languirand, *Healthy Dependency* (Newmarket, 2003), p. 19.

29 Shel Silverstein, *The Missing Piece Meets the Big O* (Harper & Row, 1981).

30 Malcolm Gladwell, *Outliers: The Story of Success* (Little, Brown, 2008), pp. 177–223.

31 From http://viewonbuddhism.org/anger.html, accessed November 2011.

32 Khalil Gibran, *The Prophet* (Knopf, 1952), p. 25.

33 Swami Vivekananda, http://thinkexist.com/quotation/do-not-stand-on-a-high-pedestal-and-take-cents-in/410962.html, accessed November 2011.

34 Saraswati Ambikananda, *Katha Upanishad* (Viking Studio, 2001).

35 Jack Kornfield, *The Wise Heart: A Guide to the Universal Teachings of Buddhist Psychology* (Bantam, 2008), pp. 167–183.

36 *The Diagnostic and Statistical Manual of Mental Disorders: DSM-IV-TR* (American Psychiatric Association, 2000).

37 From http://en.wikipedia.org/wiki/Temperament, accessed October 2011.

38 The Dalai Lama and Howard C. Cutler, *The Art of Happiness: A Handbook for Living* (Riverhead, 1998), p. 6.

39 Chogyam Trungpa, *The Heart of the Buddha* (Shambhala, 1991), p. 23.

40 Sogyal Rinpoche, Patrick Gaffney, and Andrew Harvey, *The Tibetan Book of Living and Dying* (HarperCollins, 1993), p. 47.

41   From   http://www.friendsoftheheart.com/meditation_resources/ right/bardo.shtml, adapted from various sources, including Stephen Hodge's *Illustrated Tibetan Book of the Dead*, accessed October 2011.

42   Jack Kornfield, *The Wise Heart: A Guide to the Universal Teachings of Buddhist Psychology* (Bantam, 2008), p. 1.

43   Roger Walsh and Shauna L. Shapiro, "The Meeting of Meditative Disciplines and Western Psychology: A Mutually Enriching Dialogue," *American Psychologist* 61(3): 227–239.

Printed in the USA
CPSIA information can be obtained
at www.ICGtesting.com
JSHW022220140824
68134JS00018B/1168